D1443457

"For every person struggling with harmful thoughts, this book is for you. The authors offer a triumphant guide to taking every thought captive, letting Christ renew your mind, and living in victory. Do yourself a favor and read this book. In fact, read it twice. It's that good."

> —**Wayne Cordeiro,** D.Min., founding pastor of New Hope Christian Fellowship, Honolulu, Hawaii, and bestselling author *of Leading on Empty, The Divine Mentor,* and *Doing Church as a Team*

"The authors show the reader how thoughts provide the foundations or feelings that cause us to react or respond. *Every Believer's Thought Life* shows how to transform our thinking so that our feelings and actions are transformed in the process. I love *Every Believer's Thought Life.* This book will help millions."

> —**Jacqueline Mark-Harris,** Psy.D., licensed marriage and family therapist, The Bridge Marriage and Family Therapy

"A bold and wise book for a new generation. It's easy for a person's thoughts to be hijacked in today's troubled times. *Every Believer's Thought Life* draws on God's power, modern brain science, and time-tested truths to help you set up biblical frameworks that can be applied to any problem troubling your mind. This is one of the best and most helpful books you'll read for your spiritual walk."

> —**Doug Fields,** marriage, family, and youth pastor, Mariners Church, Irvine, California

"*Every Believer's Thought Life* offers a powerful perspective on how our minds and thoughts are influenced by culture, habits, and history. Steve challenges common approaches believers often take with Scripture and offers the readers practical and meaningful takeaways which will impact their lives and, ultimately, the world around them. There is something for everyone in this book, and it will help you in your relationships, your health, and your faith."

> —**Becky L. Brown,** licensed professional clinical counselor

"What makes this book remarkable is how easy it is to read, understand, and apply to real life. No seminary-inspired jargon. No Christianese. Just page after page of helpful, Biblical guidance that will help you pursue a life of freedom and joy."
    —**David Murrow,** author of *Why Men Hate Going to Church*

"This is an excellent book. Packed with wisdom, clearly written, and full of biblical advice, *Every Believer's Thought Life* gets to the heart of the matter and surfaces what's going on inside people's hearts and minds. This book will be a game-changer for Christians everywhere."
    —**Neil Tomba,** senior pastor of Northwest Bible Church, Dallas, Texas, and author of *The Listening Road: One Man's Ride across America to Start Conversations about God*

Every Believer's Thought Life

Note: All illustrations presented in this book are true. Some names and details have been changed to protect anonymity. This publication is meant as a source of valuable information for the reader, but it is not meant as a substitute for direct, personal counseling. If such assistance is required, the services of a competent personal counselor should be sought.

EVERY BELIEVER'S THOUGHT LIFE

Defeating Destructive Mental Patterns to Gain Victory over Temptation

STEPHEN ARTERBURN AND M. N. BROTHERTON

SALEM
BOOKS
an imprint of Regnery Publishing
Washington, D.C.

THE PROMPTING:

*May the words of my mouth and the meditation of my heart
be pleasing to you, O L*ORD.

Psalm 19:14a NLT

THE PROCESS:

We take captive every thought to make it obedient to Christ.

2 Corinthians 10:5b

THE PROMISE:

You keep him in perfect peace whose mind is stayed on you.

Isaiah 26:3a ESV

CONTENTS

CHAPTER 1

Thoughts Matter

The young man across the table from me looked like what he was about to say had gotten stuck in his throat. Chase and I were meeting for coffee just to catch up, but our conversation had quickly moved on from what we'd been up to lately.

"What are you thinking?" I asked.

"Yeah, that's exactly the problem," he said with a rueful chuckle. "I've got a lot on my mind. And some of it is not so good."

Chase was a rising executive in his firm, a devoted husband, a loving father of two children, a leader in his church, and a coach in the community. Outwardly, he sure looked like he had it all together.

"Tell me more," I said.

He told me he had started following Jesus when he was a senior in high school. "My life was genuinely changed," he said. "When I first gave my life to Christ, I felt an inner peace that I had never felt before. Old habits fell away. New habits began. And the change has had lasting effects."

He paused, took a sip of coffee, and added, "I haven't looked at pornography since the day I became a Christian. Uh—certainly not every day, like I used to. Maybe once or twice a year in seventeen years. But that's it."

I nodded.

"But when I close my eyes at night…oh man." He tapped a finger against the side of his forehead. "The problem is in here. I've still got a pile of pornography right here in my mind, and I hate that!"

He said it felt like pictures from his past were holding his mind hostage. "I mean, I'm lying there next to my wife. And I love her with all my heart. But in my thoughts, I'm somewhere else. With someone else. That's just crazy and wrong! I've tried countless times to change my thought life, but the trash keeps coming back."

He looked at me dejectedly. "I don't know, Steve. Sometimes I think my internal hard drive might be permanently corrupted."

We all understand what it means to have our minds invaded by sinful thoughts and impulses. Plenty of us also understand what it feels like when occasional thoughts turn into deeply rooted patterns of thinking that bring us to the edge of despair. It doesn't have to be porn. (More on that in a minute.) For you, it might be another pattern of thinking or feeling that sometimes takes over.

Let me ask, what sort of thoughts have streamed through your mind in the last twenty-four hours? For that matter, what destructive thoughts have you meditated on and enjoyed—and repeatedly welcomed to return?

What we choose to dwell on in our minds can feel personal and embarrassing. Most of us do our best to keep it safely stashed in a mental folder marked "No big deal," or "My well-deserved private life."

But the Bible warns, "Be careful how you think; your life is shaped by your thoughts" (Proverbs 4:23 GNT). Which makes perfect sense, doesn't it? If we allow destructive thoughts to fill our mind, wouldn't we be inviting harm—and maybe deep hurt—for ourselves and those we love?

But what's a man or woman supposed to do who doesn't want to live like a hostage but can't seem to change?

If you resonate with Chase's fear that his thought life wasn't what it needed to be, even that it might have been permanently damaged, then I hope you'll keep reading. This book is for you. For years, our mission at NewLife Ministries has been to help people who find themselves trapped by trauma and sin but feel ready to reach for wholeness and freedom.

In the pages ahead, we'll draw on time-tested truths and God's power to help you identify, disarm, and take captive the unruly thought life that's been wrecking your hopes and breaking your heart. Just know that you don't need to surrender to misery ever again.

But first, let's acknowledge that your brain is an amazing thing.

Thinking Clearly about Your Thought Life

You were blessed from birth with imagination and desire, along with a host of personal preferences. And then life happened. Hurtful experiences may have powerfully shaped the way you think and feel. Like Chase, you may have found new life in Jesus only to realize that you're not quite the finished masterpiece you were hoping to be. Whatever your past, and however that might be affecting your present, I have good news. God didn't make a mistake when He made you. And if you belong to Christ, He will carry on to completion the transformation He has begun in you (see Philippians 1:7).

That includes redeeming your amazing brain. (More on that in the pages ahead, too.)

Research in cognitive neuroscience suggests that each day, "specific moments when a human is focused on a single idea" are likely to total more than six thousand.[1]

Plenty of our thoughts are harmless, of course, and some of them are certifiably wonderful. Just today, your mind solved a ridiculous parade of problems at home, work, church, or school. You tracked a host of data points for your business or a favorite sports team. You navigated complicated relationships with strangers, family, and friends. You replayed in your head pretty much exactly something you saw on TV or social media. You clearly imagined—and could already taste—that cheeseburger before you ordered.

But your mind has done more than cleverly process data. Some of your thoughts today have been good and noble. Maybe you've thought about the needs of your aging parents or a friend who's going through a hard time. You've wondered how you can be more effective at your job or in a volunteer position or how you can follow Christ wholeheartedly. Perhaps you talked to God in your mind.

---

[1] Neuroskeptic, "The 70,000 Thoughts per Day Myth?," *Discover*, May 9, 2012, https://www.discovermagazine.com/mind/the-70-000-thoughts-per-day-myth; Jason Murdock, "Humans Have More than 6,000 Thoughts per Day, Psychologists Discover," *Newsweek*, July 15, 2020, https://www.newsweek.com/humans-600 0-thoughts-every-day-1517963. The *Newsweek* article references this academic study: J. Tseng and J. Poppenk, "Brain Meta-State Transitions Demarcate Thoughts across Task Contexts Exposing the Mental Noise of Trait Neuroticism," *Nature Communications* 11, no. 3480 (July 13, 2020): https://doi.org/10.1038/s41467-020-17255-9.

Confessed sins. Gave thanks. Prayed about a need in your family or city.[2]

But you're human, so along with all the good, there's also a strong chance that random, nasty, God-dishonoring thoughts have entered your head.

Thoughts like:

- Wow, I'd like to see that person naked…
- Sheesh, I hate my supervisor so effing much!
- Ugh. I can't go to this event tonight. Everybody will be better dressed than me.
- Absolutely not fair! How come she got a bonus and I didn't?
- Hmm, I can't afford that new car, but I sure do want it. I'll buy it anyway.
- I would love to wake up with that young pastor in my bed.

Thoughts and desires like these—lust, resentment, worry, jealousy, and greed—spring from our sin natures. Yet the sins themselves mostly remain out of sight. At least to begin with.

Actually, it doesn't help that most of us look pretty good on the outside. Most of us don't rob banks or murder folks. We go through our day hoping others take what's on the outside for the real us.

Jesus, though, made a direct connection between our inner and outer lives. Take His well-known parable of two sons and a gracious father (Luke 15). The prodigal son brazenly acted out, taking

---

[2] A survey from the Pew Research Center noted that some 79 percent of Evangelicals pray every day, and another 14 percent pray weekly. See "Frequency of Prayer," Religious Landscape Study, Pew Research Center, https://www.pewforum.org/religious-landscape-study/frequency-of-prayer/.

his father's money and living it up—until he found himself broke and bunking with pigs. The elder brother, by contrast, was the super responsible son and model citizen. But inside, what a mess! He was allowing resentment, jealousy, and selfishness to poison his mind and heart and keep him isolated from his family.

In many ways, the attitudes and affections boiling up from the older son's inner core were causing as much damage to him and others as the younger son's very public, selfish actions.

Plus, Jesus strongly pointed to our need for God-honoring thoughts in Matthew 5:27–28—and for His grace when we don't have them. The Pharisees were living as if their thoughts didn't matter. They figured lustful fantasies were okay in the eyes of a holy God, as long as they weren't actually committing adultery. But Jesus pointed to the condition of their minds. He surfaced the duplicity, saying it indeed matters what's going on inside a person's inner core. Although Jesus was speaking to men on this occasion, His teaching applies to women, too.

The Mind-Heart Connection

What exactly is this inner core of ours that warrants so much attention?

Biblically, the term "heart" (*lebab* in Hebrew and *kardia* in Greek[3]) is used metaphorically as the source of emotions, beliefs, cravings, and thoughts. A person's heart and mind combine to

---

[3] *Strong's Hebrew Lexicon*, (H3824) "lēbāb," Blue Letter Bible, https://www.blueletterbible.org/lexicon/h3824/kjv/wlc/o-1/. The word is defined as "the heart (as the most interior organ)," "bethink themselves, breast, comfortably, courage, midst, mind, unawares," and "understanding"; *Strong's Greek Lexicon*, (G2588) "kardia," Blue Letter Bible, https://www.blueletterbible.org/lexicon/g2588/kjv/tr/o-1/. The lexicon states that the word is rendered "the heart, i.e. (figuratively); the thoughts or feelings (mind); also (by analogy) the middle."

make us who we are. We see it described in 1 Chronicles 28:9, as the young King Solomon is encouraged to serve God "with a willing mind," because "the LORD searches every heart and understands every desire and every thought." Here we get a clear sense that our hearts and minds are closely wound together in our inner being.

We see the mind-heart connection revealed beautifully in the life of Mary. The Bible says that after the birth of Jesus and the announcement by angels that a Savior had been born, his mother "treasured up all these things and pondered them in her heart" (Luke 2:19). There it is again—thoughts and desires treasured and pondered, working together with great power to drive actions.

No wonder Scripture calls us to love God with every part of our being—all our heart, mind, soul, and strength (Mark 12:30–31).

Like Mary, and with Christ's power in our hearts and minds, we can enjoy the deep sense of peace and confidence that emerges as we "take captive every thought to make it obedient to Christ" (2 Corinthians 10:5). We'll explore all of this in depth in chapters to come. Friend, the battle for your thought life can be won.

On-Air Confessions

We led with the problem of pornography in this book for a reason. For so many men and women these days, that's the fire burning in the attic. It used to be considered more of a men's problem only. But the number of women using porn is on the rise. Research shows that in the general population, nine out of ten adult men and six out of ten women have viewed porn in the past month. The numbers for Christians are lower, but certainly not as low as you'd hope.[4] In fact, on our *NewLife Live!* radio broadcast, the majority of phone calls that we get from listeners—who are virtually all Christian—center around porn. People want to know how to get free from this scourge. If they're not struggling with porn themselves, they want to know how to help friends and loved ones who are.

For you, the battles in your mind might come in other areas. If that's the case, you're not alone. At *NewLife Live!* we are blessed with thousands of thoughtful, honest, and big-hearted listeners who sincerely want to follow Christ more closely. If you're not a regular listener, you might be surprised to learn what Christians say when the microphone is on. Many reveal their inner lives to be, well, a mess. A minefield of mental hazards where "new life in Christ" is not much in evidence.

For example:

- Rage. For some, their minds are like tornadoes, swirling with angry thoughts. Sometimes they can't control their anger. They might be walking through a perfectly fine day when an incident triggers their rage and they explode. They wonder, "Whoa, where did that come from?"

---

[4] Statistics on general populations show that some 91.5 percent of all adult men and 60.2 percent of women have viewed porn in the past month. For Christians, the numbers are lower, although trickier to definitively calculate due to variants in the definition of "Christian," as a recent article in the Gospel Coalition showed, which is why we didn't include them in the text. Still, the numbers are not encouraging. See I. Solano, N. Eaton, and K. O'Leary, "Pornography Consumption, Modality and Function in a Large Internet Sample," *The Journal of Sex Research* 57, no. 1 (January 2020): 92–103, https://doi.org/10.1080/00224499.2018.1532488; Joe Carter, "FactChecker: Do Christian Men Watch More Pornography?," The Gospel Coalition Current Affairs, June 8, 2020, https://www.thegospelcoalition.org/article/factchecker-do-christian-men-watch-more-pornography/.

- Envy. Maybe they're on social media a lot, constantly comparing their life to someone else's. They see endless pictures of perfect smiles, happy families, glorious vacations, and big accomplishments. They lose themselves in obsessing over what others have.
- Anxiety. I'm not talking about clinical anxiety often rooted in trauma, which requires specialized treatment. I'm talking about the regular, bothersome kind of worry that can happen whenever we don't know the outcome of a situation. But for these folks, it's become a deeply ingrained pattern of suffering.
- Grudges. Someone hurt them, and resentment sets in. A conflict-filled conversation, often rooted in something else that happened long ago, is constantly being replayed in their mind.
- Chronic negativity. I'm not talking about occasional irritability. Chronically negative people are filled with grumbling and complaining. They seem to falsely think it's their responsibility to criticize everything. Church. Friends. Family members. The school system. Themselves.
- Rigid polarization. Seems like more Christians than ever can think only in black-and-white terms. Us or them. My way or the highway. Gone is cooperation. Forbearance. Nuance. For them, there's no loving a neighbor if that neighbor thinks differently than they do.
- Weak and immature thinking. I'm not sure what else to call it, but it causes great harm. Perhaps the person jumps to faulty conclusions. They are suspicious without reason. They take one bit of information and

create a faulty narrative around it. Somebody didn't
return a phone call, so that person hates them. They
wore a new sweater to work, but nobody noticed, so
they conclude that all coworkers dislike them.

Even for sincere, well-intentioned believers, habits of mind like
these can cause a world of hurt when they go unchallenged by
truth. Thankfully, every one of these thought patterns is a learned
response that can be unlearned. With our willingness and the
power of the Holy Spirit, they can be refashioned and redeemed.

What happens when even epically gifted people of God don't
let the truth do its work?

Consider the lives of three biblical standouts: Samson, David,
and Solomon. You probably know their stories well.

When Thoughts Become Actions

All three started out with so much promise. All had ample
spiritual resources at their disposal. All flourished for a time. Yet
all fell hard.

Samson was at the front end of a stellar career. As a mighty war-
rior and national leader, he singlehandedly humiliated the Philistines,
Israel's enemies, time and again. Yet his mind was clouded by defi-
ance and lust. He went looking for trouble in an enemy town and
found it in an attractive Philistine woman. He returned to his parents
with a demand: "Get her for me as my wife." When his parents tried
to talk sense to him, he upped his insolence: "Get her for me, for she
is right in my eyes" (Judges 14:1–3 ESV).

His lust-fueled, risk-taking behavior continued until he
famously came to grief at the hands of a Philistine mistress
named Delilah.

Over decades of wholeheartedly serving God, David had led Israel to prosperity and security despite intense opposition. Yet at the height of his career, he chose the easy way out, allowing his mind to give in to laziness and lust. In the springtime, we're told, when kings went off to do their jobs protecting their nations, David shirked his duty and stayed home in Jerusalem (2 Samuel 11:1). That offered him prime opportunity to watch a married woman bathing on her rooftop. His private indulgence led to a pregnancy and the murder of her husband.

Solomon became known far and wide for his brilliance, but his mind harbored a contradictory mix of insight and idolatry. He began his kingship by praying for wisdom (1 Kings 3:1–14), and much was given. God's wisdom could have safeguarded him and preserved his life from sin, if only he had heeded his own advice. But the richer and more powerful he became, the more he lost his grip on wise living. Astonishingly, he ended up having seven hundred wives and three hundred concubines, most of whom worshipped idols. The Bible says that "as Solomon grew old, his wives turned his heart after other gods" (1 Kings 11:1).

Where did each of these powerful and gifted people go wrong?

In their minds.

For them, passing impulses became habits. Loyalties in their core shifted. Soon, appealing but toxic thought patterns—which no doubt sounded like jewels of wisdom at the time—led them to defeat.

Of course, some people these days insist there's nothing wrong with dwelling upon an illicit thought, as long as they don't act on it. We should let our minds think any thoughts we want, they insist, and then entertain those thoughts as frequently or as long as we wish. Illicit thoughts are actually good for us, they claim. Those thoughts promote personal happiness and will actually help marital fidelity, they contend. If we think about an affair, for example, we're less likely to act on it. That's the logic.

Just listen to this nugget of lousy advice:

> We run into problems when we start suppressing and running away from our desires, because that's how we lose control of them and they start controlling us. Suppressing sexual thoughts can lead to an obsessive preoccupation with them that ultimately harms our mental health.[5]

Oh, good grief!

What if a person has sexual fantasies about molesting a child? What if a person continually imagines raping someone? What happens when a decent man or woman "treasures" in their heart a romantic or sexual choice that would ruin a marriage or a career? The key to good mental health is certainly not to allow and encourage harmful fantasies.

Note the deliberately pejorative words used in the previous quote. My friend, God does not call anybody to "suppress" their sexual thoughts, in the sense of stuffing those thoughts deep inside, never to be honestly examined or dealt with. God does not call anyone to "run away" from their desires, unless those desires contradict His revealed will. On the contrary, God is the Grand Designer of libidos, body parts, sexual desire, and procreation. He champions human sexuality and invites people to lovingly express themselves within safeguarded parameters.

---

[5] "How the Science of Sexual Desire Can Improve Your Sex Life: A Q&A with Justin Lehmiller, Ph.D.," Goop, https://goop.com/wellness/sexual-health/how-the-science-of-sexual-desire-can-improve-your-sex-life/.

Most well-credentialed researchers, both secular and faith-based, do indeed caution that some fantasies can be harmful—and that lines up with what the Bible teaches, too. We should not welcome or entertain every thought that pops into our minds. Consider this sound bit of advice from Dr. Lynn Margolies, psychologist and former Harvard Medical School faculty member:

> Fantasizing about another person may seem like a harmless indulgence, but it actually draws us closer to temptation and can increase the risk of being unfaithful.
>
> In the same way that dwelling on worries and possible catastrophes fuels anxiety and makes fears more vivid, immersion in fantasy can enhance, rather than quench, our longings.
>
> Fantasy provides the fuel for affairs. It helps lead up to them, it perpetuates them, and it makes it difficult to back away or let go.[6]

Fantasies are not harmless. Think infidelity could never happen to you? Dr. Margolies adds that the people who have affairs are often

> [C]onventional, well-meaning, and moral, often with lifelong histories of unidentified emotional neglect.
>
> Their ingrained patterns of being overly responsible, self-sacrificing and accommodating make them especially vulnerable to needing to break out and seek relief from a feeling of burden and lack of vitality.

---

[6] Lynn Margolies, "When Fantasy Crosses the Line," Psych Central, May 17, 2016, https://psychcentral.com/lib/when-fantasy-crosses-the-line#1.

As their weakened threshold of restraint is overwhelmed by temptation, it's not long before they are
headed for a freefall.[7]

It's not rocket science to see how illicit fantasies can turn into
illicit behavior. It's simply the nature at work, and the Bible warns
that "you will always harvest what you plant" (Galatians 6:7 NLT).

Even with the Best of Intentions

One early morning at an out-of-town conference, Jessica decides
that when lunch is served, she'll skip dessert. For one thing, she's
on a health kick. For another, she wants to be mentally sharp for
the afternoon sessions.

Lunchtime arrives. Jessica expects to be directed through a
buffet line, where she can choose her meal from among the offer-
ings. Instead, she and all three hundred attendees are led to another
room and seated at round tables. Caterers appear laden with trays
of pre-plated meals, and they proceed to plunk plates down in front
of each attendee.

Jessica eats the meal. It's grilled chicken with steamed broccoli
and seasoned potatoes. Not bad on a health scale. But twenty
minutes later, the caterers file out of the kitchen again and before
anyone can decline, they plunk a slice of cheesecake in front of each
attendee.

Jessica stares at the dessert in front of her. She stares hard. She
hasn't chosen what she is seeing. In fact, she had deliberately
decided to go the other direction. But the whipped cream looks so
smooth. So velvety. There it sits—cheesecake!—right before her

---

[7] Ibid.

eyes. She doesn't really want to eat it. She doesn't need it. But dessert is playing offense.

She eats the cheesecake. These things happen, right? In the heat of the moment, resolves weaken. In fact, studies have shown that willpower isn't all it's cracked up to be. Willpower is actually a limited resource, becoming depleted along with our energy levels throughout the day.[8]

Fast-forward to Jessica's hotel room that evening. She reviews her notes, calls her husband and children to say goodnight, and settles in to watch some TV before sleep.

Before she ever left home, she had resolved that she wouldn't watch anything illicit on TV. As a matter of best practices for business and life, she runs family filters on her laptop and phone. Plus, she's a woman of integrity and she knows that pornography dishonors God and her spouse, wastes time, and destroys self-respect.

But when she turns on the TV in her hotel room, two viewing options immediately pop up. The first is for regular channels. The second is for "adult entertainment"—and she can see there's a specially designed romantic section just for women.

Jessica stares at those two options like she'd stared at the pre-plated cheesecake. She stares hard. She'd already decided to say no. But the option has been plunked down on the screen right in front of her. Tonight, porn is playing offense...

Ever been there?

We live in such challenging times for guarding our minds. I can remember the days before the internet. In that era, no God-honoring Christ-follower would have stashed a pornographic

---

[8] Jon Tierney, "Do You Suffer from Decision Fatigue?," *New York Times Magazine*, August 17, 2011, http://www.nytimes.com/2011/08/21/magazine/do-you-suffer-from-decision-fatigue.html?_r=2&pagewanted=all.

magazine in his desk drawer at work. No serious believer would have willingly kept porn in her purse. It was so much harder then to hide duplicity—and besides, the temptation would have seemed much too close.

These days, however, the temptations come pre-plated. Anyone with a laptop or smart phone has unlimited access to pornography every second of every day. You wanted a phone so you could text your friends and family, but it came with a heap of trash installed. You wanted a laptop so you could write your reports for work, but with it came a river of harm. The pornography is always present, always waiting, always available.

Even with the best of intentions, you and I are under attack.

Naming the Assailants

Fortunately, that night at the hotel, Jessica doesn't fill her mind with anything destructive. She has the good sense to move on, no matter how mentally tired she is and how seductively the adult channels might beckon. Yet the incident serves as a reminder that we seldom go out and look for temptation. More often, temptation finds us. And we've known from ancient times how that happens.

The Bible names the three main assailants—the world, the flesh, and the devil (Ephesians 2:1–3).

"The world" is the catchall term for people and subcultures that aren't committed to following God. Peer pressure can happen at any age, and if our minds are being influenced by the world, then temptation and sin can result. The Apostle John warns, "Do not love the world or anything in the world" (1 John 2:15). Note that the phrase "love the world" is used here in a different sense than John 3:16, where we're told that "God so loved the world." The latter connotes an honorable concern for the welfare of all people. The former implies an unhealthy love for destructive things. Our call is to avoid the former.

"The flesh" is shorthand for the physical and emotional cravings we all experience, even though we follow Jesus. You're trying to comfort, reward, or soothe yourself after a hard day, so you consume substances or pursue behaviors that may not be healthy in the long run. You're just doing what your mind or heart is asking for, and it's easy to shrug it off with, "It's okay if I give in just this one time." But the struggle isn't going anywhere. The Apostle Paul was alluding to his own struggles with the flesh when he lamented, "I want to do what is right, but I don't do it. Instead, I do what I hate" (Romans 7:15 NLT). Our natural tendency is to indulge the flesh. But life teaches us (beginning with parents, teachers, and coaches) that though brainless, the flesh is mighty. It takes smart decisions and plenty of willpower to harness fleshly desires for a higher good. Like doing our homework, winning in sports, staying off drugs, or just getting out of bed.

"The devil," also called Satan, is not a red-horned cartoon character but a very real enemy who "prowls around like a roaring lion looking for someone to devour" (1 Peter 5:8–9). Paul describes the devil and his legions as "the spiritual forces of evil" that fiercely oppose every believer (Ephesians 6:12).

Jesus called the devil a thief who comes only to steal, kill, and destroy (John 10:10a). He tries to steal from us whatever is valuable, prized, or cherished. He wants to kill anything that's alive and full of God-ordained purpose. He wants to destroy everything in our thoughts that pertains to a healthy, God-honoring life, family, reputation, ministry, and future.

By the way, our spiritual enemy doesn't care when or where our life blows up. Samson was young when he fell. David was middle-aged. Solomon was in his senior years. The devil can be patient as an ox, as slow-moving as an iceberg. He is "a liar and the father of lies" (John 8:44)—and his influence might be encountered in the media we watch, the company we keep, the cravings we desire, or the lies we hear and repeat to ourselves. As pastor C. Haynes Jr. writes, "Satan is a thought influencer. The reason Satan seeks to influence your thoughts is because he knows that [your mind] is your control center."[9]

It's important to note Satan's limitations. For instance, he is not everywhere at the same time. He's not omnipresent like God is. Due to the sheer number of people on Earth, it's unlikely that Satan himself is targeting you, even though his influence can show up anywhere. Satan and his demons can't read our minds, and they can't indwell a believer to influence the mind from the inside out. We are temples of the living God, and the Holy Spirit alone indwells us (2 Corinthians 6:15–16).

One of my favorite verses is 1 John 4:4: "Greater is he that is in you, than he that is in the world" (KJV). Satan might be a formidable opponent, but Christ is far greater than Satan—and we have Christ. Thanks to Jesus, Hell is defeated. Death does not have the final say. The ultimate war is already won.

Yes, there are plenty of skirmishes left to fight—not just with porn and illicit sexual fantasies, but with any troubling thoughts that fill our mind—and that's why it's so important to stay vigilant. In Christ, we have the weapons we need for victory. We can "be strong in the Lord" and "put on the full armor of God" so that we can take a stand against the devil's schemes (Ephesians 6:10–11). We are told to "be alert and of sober mind" (1 Peter 5:8–9), to "resist

---

[9] Clarence L. Haynes Jr., "Can Satan Read Our Minds?," Crosswalk.com, October 7, 2021, https://www.crosswalk.com/faith/spiritual-life/can-satan-read-our-minds.html.

the devil" (James 4:7) and to "pray in the Spirit on all occasions" (Ephesians 6:18).

I hope you're noticing that the new life we so desperately need and want begins with a renewed mind that is God's eternal promise and our unchangeable inheritance. That's why you and I can boldly face our assailants and reach out for new beginnings in Christ's name.

A Place to Begin

As we choose to align with the heart of God and let His truth change us, the holiness of Christ is able to cover every aspect of our lives, even the most humbling struggle.

By the end of this book, you'll have a complete picture of how God brings healing and strength in the areas where you struggle most. We stress the word "complete." You might have noticed some books teach you how to target isolated issues such as lust or worry. But this book will show you how to set up biblical frameworks that can be applied to any problem troubling your mind. The benefits are far-reaching and full.

- You'll discover how to get rid of all "mental muck" and replace it with "God thoughts." New Testament writers like the apostles Paul and James describe this transformational process as a kind of great exchange—war for peace, dishonor for honor, old mind for new mind.
- You'll learn how to step confidently into your new, real identity in Christ. What does it mean to be a chosen son or daughter of God? In very practical ways, who you and I are really can make all the difference in what's possible by grace.

- You'll discover the surprising power of what one famous theologian called "the expulsive power of a new affection." Fascinating, I promise—and life-changing.
- We'll check under the hood, so to speak, and ask what's wrong. What's injured or broken in our inner core, and what could you do next to get into finely tuned, working order?
- You'll be coached in how, like a trained athlete, you can tap into the abundant power of scriptural truth to experience outcomes you may have thought were beyond you.
- You'll learn how to build what I call a "structurally wise life."
- We'll talk frankly about what good thinking about sex looks like in a believer's life, because God means it to be one of His best gifts. Why let the world, the flesh, and the devil rob us?
- And you'll discover how to unleash the power and favor of Heaven in your marriage and personal life.

But all of that is to come. Right here, right now at the start, I invite you to take a simple but life-changing step. Will you commit to praying for something that God always answers yes to? Ten times out of ten. A billion times out of a billion.

It's the prayer for wisdom.

James 1:5 says, "If any of you lacks wisdom, you should ask God, who gives generously to all without finding fault, and it will be given to you."

Note the last words. "It will be given to you." It's a guarantee— again and again. Due to this promise, you can pray for wisdom every day of your life, from this point forward.[10] You have a biblical assurance that God's wisdom will be given to you. Imagine you're at the end of your days, looking back on your life. Each day of your life from this point to that point will be marked by wisdom.

Ask God for wisdom right now, my friend. Your prayer doesn't need to be fancy. It might be a simple as: *Lord Jesus, according to Your promise, please give me wisdom.*

From this point forward, every day, wisdom is available. You will have wisdom for how you talk and act. You will have wisdom for your hopes and desires. You will have wisdom for your secret struggles. You will have wisdom for your friendships, relationships, marriage, education, work, hobbies, volunteer efforts, and plans. You will have wisdom in love, in faith, and in integrity.

Most importantly, since everything will flow from this, you will have wise thoughts.

Key Takeaways

- It matters what we think. Sin is sin, and any moment spent in sin—mentally or otherwise—is squandered time. Sin dishonors God and robs us of life's best. Fortunately, with Christ's power working within us, we can take charge of our thought life and enjoy the deep sense of peace and confidence that emerges when our mind is wholly focused on God and His best for our life.
- The solution to winning the battles in our mind involves the exchange of illicit thoughts for Christ-honoring thoughts. But that can be easier said

---

[10] Thanks to Shelley Giglio for clarifying the idea of praying for wisdom every day.

than done. Watch out! Three forces war against every believer—the world, the flesh, and the devil. Plus, even if we're not seeking illicit thoughts, those thoughts can be ushered to us, putting us on the defense.

- Willpower is important, but it's not enough, because it can diminish over time. A solution begins when we pray for God's wisdom to permeate our minds—each and every day. Further solutions will be explained as the book unfolds.

CHAPTER 2

Go to Your God-Thought

We had a dream. My coauthor and I wanted to create a children's book that made it fun for kids to learn about Jesus. And we wouldn't stop at just one book. We hoped to create an entire series.

We prayed and brainstormed, planned and talked. We carefully wrote a book proposal, and our agent shopped it within the industry and secured a contract with a well-established publisher. We researched and wrote the manuscript, editing it again and again. We ran test markets with kids and their parents, and all the early feedback was favorable. The book went through the entire editing process with the publisher. A fantastic illustrator drew the pictures. An amazing voice actor recorded the audio version. Finally, after three long years, the book was published. It had a cool title and an even cooler subtitle: *Kirby McCook and the Jesus Chronicles: A 12-Year-Old's Take on the Totally Unboring,*

Slightly Weird Stuff in the Bible, Including Fish Guts, Wrestling Moves, and Stinky Feet.

Readers loved the book. They gave it many five-star reviews.

Max Lucado endorsed it, saying, "Your kids will laugh and learn, and ultimately grow closer to the Savior. I highly recommend this book!"

Parents, grandparents, and children's pastors emailed us, saying how much they appreciated it. They talked about how kids were devouring *Kirby McCook and the Jesus Chronicles*, meeting the Jesus of the Bible in new and good ways.

We marketed the book, recorded podcasts and radio spots, wrote articles, and sent out copies to key influencers. We held book signings and attended children's ministry conferences to help spread the word.

The publishing industry noticed. *Kirby McCook and the Jesus Chronicles* was nominated for the Evangelical Christian Publishers Association's Christian Book Awards. And we won! Our book received the gold medallion of excellence in the Young People's Literature category. In the world of faith-based books, that's like winning an Oscar.

But...

(Did you sense a "but" was coming?)

Despite the buzz, our book sold poorly. The publisher said, "Thanks, but no thanks" to a sequel; a series wasn't going to happen. The publishing industry is a business, after all, and it's not uncommon for well-received, critically acclaimed books to fall through the cracks. We prayed and asked God to intervene. But the door was closed.

How did I feel?

Disappointed.

When people feel disappointed, their thoughts may do acrobatics, and not all of the gyrations are beneficial. I prayed and brainstormed and had several long talks with my coauthor, agent, and trusted friends. That helped, but still I was frustrated.

How about you? When was the last time you felt disappointed? In what direction did your thoughts turn?

Flip the Framework

Compared to the disappointments some people experience, I realize that having a book sell poorly is certainly not catastrophic. Yet suffering sits on a relative scale. When you hope for something and it doesn't happen, when you see a dream wither and die, or when you value something and it's lost or taken away, disappointment is the most natural response. The emotion of disappointment acts as an umbrella that encompasses many other feelings, including dismay, grief, anger, frustration, sorrow, fear, regret, guilt, and loss. Regardless of the severity of hardship in the events that prompted the feeling, disappointment is a valid emotion.

As an antidote for disappointment, we need our minds to be restored. Something has been lost, and now it needs to be rebuilt. We need healing. We need the disappointment removed and something hopeful put in its place. How can we be restored from any disappointment great or small?

Start by flipping the framework. Disappointment can fade with time, but if it doesn't, a pattern occurs in our thought life. Sometimes it plays out in behavior, too. Let's call this "the Pattern of Mental Muck" so we can easily remember it. Pause a moment to honestly take stock and fill in these blanks as they pertain to you. The Pattern of Mental Muck goes like this:

A. I experienced disappointment when this happened: _____.

B. Because of that disappointment, I sought comfort, soothing, relief, or restoration.

C. I turned toward _____ to comfort, soothe, relieve, or restore me.

Part A of the pattern is a universal human experience. Everybody goes through disappointment to some degree, although the specific circumstances change from person to person.

Part B is also a given. No one likes to feel disappointed. From a biological perspective, the experience of disappointment triggers the stress hormone cortisol to flood the body,[1] while a part of our brain called the habenula goes into overdrive.[2] As our brains work to cope with the loss, our thoughts may turn fuzzy, and in times of extreme disappointment, our logic and powers of reasoning may take a hit. It's easy to feel overwhelmed, sad, disoriented, or confused.[3] That prompts us to seek respite and healing. Naturally, we want what's been lost to be restored.

With Part C, people turn to something for comfort—and this is the key piece of the framework that may need to be flipped. A person might turn toward a helpful activity such as exercising, talking to a friend, or journaling in an attempt to sort out their thoughts. That's good, and those activities don't factor into the Muck. But a person might also turn toward things that are harmful,

---

[1] Mary-Frances O'Connor, "Grief: A Brief History of Research on How Body, Mind, and Brain Adapt," *Psychosomatic Medicine* 81, no. 8 (October 2019): 731–8, https://doi.org/10.1097/PSY.0000000000000717.

[2] Ju Tian and Nao Uchida, "Pathway for Disappointment [Uchida Lab]," Harvard University Department of Molecular and Cellular Biology, September 10, 2015, https://www.mcb.harvard.edu/department/news/pathway-for-disappointment-uchida-lab/.

[3] April Reese, "The Fog of Grief," *Aeon*, August 10, 2021, https://aeon.co/essays/how-the-brain-responds-to-grief-can-change-who-we-are.

such as alcohol—a numbing substance that disrupts neurotransmitters in the brain[4]—or toward a new but unhealthy relationship, or toward habitual grumbling or complaining, or toward a default mindset of anger or dismay, or possibly toward a seductive but ultimately harmful mental image that replays over and over. That part of the pattern needs to be flipped.

A woman emailed our resource center asking for help. We steered her in a helpful direction, and about a month later she emailed back, saying she was doing much better. She offered to let us use her story if it could help somebody else. She wrote:

> *I need a little tough love for my wandering mind. I'm a Christian, and I always try to do the right thing, but I admit that my go-to mental calmer or pick-me-up is always some kind of romantic or sexual fantasy.*
>
> *By way of example, I'll be sitting in a dentist chair getting my teeth cleaned. It's uncomfortable, so I'll picture something sexy that I've seen or read about. Since I'm concentrating on that image or storyline, I'm not thinking about the discomfort anymore.*
>
> *I might be bored, waiting to pick my daughter up from dance class, so I'll start thinking sexy thoughts. Mentally, I'll be far away.*
>
> *If I can't fall asleep at night, I picture a romantic scene, one that's more calming than sexy, and that lulls me to sleep.*
>
> *I was in a staff meeting at work when two of my coworkers got into this big disagreement about a campaign. I hate conflict, so I brought up a sexual image*

---

[4] E. Sullivan, R. Adron Harris, and A. Pfefferbaum, "Alcohol's Effects on Brain and Behavior," *Alcohol Research and Health* 33, no. 1–2 (2010): 127–43, https://www.ncbi.nlm.nih.gov/pmc/articles/PMC3625995/.

*in my head and zoned out, right there at the confer-
ence table.*

*I should mention that none of these images are about
my husband. That's what I regret so much. We love each
other, but he doesn't enter my fantasies anymore. I don't
want to act upon my daydreams. Even so, what should
I do?*

Notice the Pattern of Mental Muck? The illicit mental escapism
happened when she was uncomfortable, bored, restless, or in the
middle of a conflict. All those experiences could be described as
"disappointing" times. In seeking comfort, she turned to illicit
thoughts.

When we slip into any kind of Mental Muck, we tend to dig
deeper and deeper. But yes, there is a way out. Hebrews 12:1–2
offers an important new framework to help us flip the Pattern of
Mental Muck and enjoy the peace and confidence that emerges
when our minds are fully focused on Christ. Hebrews 12:1–2 is
not the only answer Scripture provides, but it gets us started with
its beautiful and clear example of what restoration looks like:

That's because Hebrews was written to people going through
hard times. They were familiar with disappointment, grief,
and loss. The writer of Hebrews comes alongside them in an
arm-around-shoulder style and says, "There is encouragement—
it's available today, and it's available tomorrow, and it's available
after that."

Therefore, since we are surrounded by such a great cloud
of witnesses, let us throw off everything that hinders and
the sin that so easily entangles. And let us run with perseverance the race marked out for us, fixing our eyes on

Jesus, the pioneer and perfecter of faith. For the joy set
before him he endured the cross, scorning its shame, and
sat down at the right hand of the throne of God. (NIV)

To clarify, the encouragement and advice in Hebrews is not
"self-help" in the sense that everything depends on us and our
superhuman efforts. Deep and lasting life change ultimately comes
from God. His power is grace-oriented and divinely fueled, and
He does the greatest work in our life. Always keep in mind that
the true power to change comes from Him.

How do we know this? Paul writes in Ephesians 3:20 that we
are strengthened "according to His power that is at work within
us," and in 2 Corinthians 4:16 he points out that by Christ's power
"we are being renewed day by day." Philippians 2:13 states that "it
is God who works in you to will and to act in order to fulfill his
good purpose." These statements all reflect the supernatural work
of God.

Yet we do have a responsibility to welcome God's work. We
must agree with His transformation as it's happening. We must not
resist the change He brings. Rather, we want to diligently lean in
and commit to the work He's doing in us.

Paul tells the believers in Corinth that spiritual life is like a race
we must run to win (1 Corinthians 9:24–27). He encourages the
believers in Philippi to press onward and strain forward toward the
goal (Philippians 3:12–14). Three times, the Apostle Peter exhorts
believers to "make every effort" in our spiritual lives (2 Peter 1:5,
10, and 3:14). Notice in each verse that our work is required. The
ultimate power to change comes from God, yet we have responsibility in the process.

With this responsibility in mind, let's take a closer look at
the key passage, Hebrews 12:1–2. Note three grace-filled,

God-empowered actions we can take as we partner with God in our restoration to change the channels in our mind. How do we, using God's power, invite Christ to overturn the Pattern of Mental Muck for us? Remember that these actions can help cleanse our minds, not just of illicit sexual thoughts, but of *any* harmful thought—be it negativity, an overextended need to be in control, fear, perfectionism, envy, rage, grudges, rigid polarization, and more.

First, Throw Off All Hindrances and Entanglements

Picture yourself wearing a heavy overcoat on a summer day. You throw off the overcoat, cast it aside, and refrain from putting it on again. The first part of Hebrews 12:1–2 urges us to "throw off everything that hinders and the sin that so easily entangles." This action of throwing off sin primarily happens in our thought life—although it can happen in our actions, too.

Hebrews reminds us that it's easy to pick up the heavy coat of sin and put it on. Sin tells us a big lie, saying that if we turn toward things that harm us, we will feel better.

"Come to me," the porn hisses, "and I will give you rest."

"Indulge in me," the resentment croons, "and I will make you feel better."

"Spend some time with me," calls bitterness, "and I will give you that pick-me-up you're looking for. I will lull you to sleep. I will soothe you in the midst of conflict."

All lies!

When we are disappointed, the initial negative emotion we feel isn't wrong. Jesus wept, experienced loneliness, and grew frustrated with His disciples more than once. Whenever we are disappointed, grieved, angry, hungry, tired, or lonely, it's not wrong to feel the truth of those emotions. But where we go with those negative emotions makes a big difference in our spiritual life.

If we want true restoration, then we must challenge and cast off the Pattern of Mental Muck. When we are disappointed, it does us no good to turn to that which hinders and entangles us. By contrast, 2 Corinthians 1:3–4a indicates that God is "the Father of compassion and the God of all comfort, who comforts us in all our troubles." And 1 Peter 5:7 invites us to "cast all our anxiety on Him, because He cares for us."

Notice the flipped framework for restoration. Whenever we experience disappointment and loss, instead of turning to sin, we can pray, filling our minds with something like this:

> *Lord Jesus, You said that You're the God of all comfort.*
> *So I don't want to go to that which hinders me. I don't*
> *want to look for soothing in the sin that so easily entan-*
> *gles. In the same breath that I'm lamenting this disap-*
> *pointment, I'm running to You for comfort. You say in*
> *Your Word that I can cast all anxiety upon You because*
> *You care for me. Lord, by Your grace and power, help*
> *me do that. I want to be restored, so I turn to You.*

It's not always easy to pray. Jesus surely understands this.

A friend and his wife recently went through an extremely difficult season with one of their children. Great trauma was inflicted upon their family, and my friend told me that when the hardship first came into their lives, he could barely sleep at night. Here's how he described it:

> My mind was absolutely racing. I could barely think,
> much less pray. Far in the back of my thoughts was a

verse I'd memorized long ago. I couldn't remember the whole verse, and I felt too exhausted and staggered by the news of what had happened to get up, turn on a light, and look it up. But I recalled that Jesus was talking to His disciples, offering comfort, and that He promised peace.

Those first several nights, I lay awake, praying two words from that verse. Over and over again, I prayed, "Jesus, peace. Jesus, peace." I regulated my breathing to the prayer and it became automatic. When I inhaled, I prayed, "Jesus." When I exhaled, I prayed, "peace." That was my only prayer. I couldn't think of any other words to pray. I just needed to drill that truth into me—that Jesus was with me, and that Jesus offered peace.

As difficult as the experience was for that family, my friend's response was good. He didn't have the whole verse in his mind, at least not so he could recite it fully, but he grasped enough of it to focus his thoughts on Christ and pray. He didn't succumb to the Pattern of Mental Muck. How much more would his problems have been compounded if he'd gotten up, flipped open his laptop, and indulged in porn?

Praying only a few words is perfectly fine. The Holy Spirit translates in our times of weakness. "We do not know what we ought to pray for, but the Spirit himself intercedes for us through wordless groans" (Romans 8:26).

Incidentally, the full verse my friend was trying to recall is John 14:27, when Jesus said, "Peace I leave with you; my peace I give you. I do not give to you as the world gives. Do not let your hearts be troubled and do not be afraid."

That's a new pattern at work. Do you want to win the battles in your mind? Don't give in to sin. Instead, pray. Turn to Christ. It's so simple we almost miss it.

Second, Run with Perseverance

The next part of Hebrews 12:1–2 encourages us to "run with perseverance the race marked out for us."

The word "perseverance" is key. Life is hard. When the going gets tough, our inclination may be to walk out the side door. This disposition happens in our thoughts first, and then we act. The difficulty might exist in a marriage, work situation, or ministry. The struggle is real, and the hardship is taking its toll.

One caveat here: certainly, if a difficult situation turns abusive or toxic, then we need to create boundaries, leave, and safeguard ourselves and families.[5] Yet within the regular course of life, God often calls us to stay in a hard situation—at least for a time.

God is never the author of evil, but perhaps Jesus wants us in a difficult situation for a particular reason. He wants us to wait for His timing before we move on. Instead of quitting or walking away, our task is to ask God what He wants us to do within that hard situation. Hebrews 10:36 and 39 say, "You need to persevere so that when you have done the will of God, you will receive what he has promised," and "We do not belong to those who shrink back and are destroyed, but to those who have faith and are saved."

Perhaps God wants us to stay in a hard job because we are the only salt and light in that office. Every time we are with our difficult

---

[5] For a helpful resource on toxicity and boundary setting, see Gary Thomas, *When to Walk Away* (Grand Rapids, Michigan: Zondervan, 2019).

boss, we're praying for him in our mind. *Oh Lord, help this guy. He needs you, just like I need you.* Marriages can be difficult for any number of reasons, but perhaps God wants us to stay the course so the adversity helps us become the spouse we need to be. Ministries can experience challenges, but maybe God wants us to stay because He's going to lead everybody through a hard time as a team to build strength and depth. During that hardship, we're going to grow in faith and praise Him in the storm.

The Greek word for perseverance is *hypomonē*.[6] It connotes cheerful endurance, particularly when facing affliction or suffering. The trait is characteristic of someone "who is not swerved from his deliberate purpose and his loyalty to faith by even the greatest trials and sufferings."[7] Someone running a race experiences discomfort. He is hot, sweaty, and tired. He wants to stop running but needs to persevere. In one carefully chosen word, he is experiencing *inconvenience*.

That might seem strange for a word choice, but think of it this way: Running is not the most convenient mode of travel. The runner could ride a bike or take a car. For conveying a message, far more convenient ways exist. The runner could pick up the phone or send a text.

Running is inconvenient, and when we run, we are required to have this Greek trait of *hypomonē*—cheerful perseverance. The runner deliberately chooses to be hot, sweaty, and tired because he is running for other reasons than transportation or communication. He has his eyes on a different prize altogether.

The same mindset is needed in our thought life. When it comes to throwing off sin, we must be willing to be inconvenienced for

---

[6] *Strong's Greek Lexicon*, (G5281) "hypomonē," Blue Letter Bible, https://www.blueletterbible.org/lexicon/g5281/kjv/tr/0-1/.

[7] Ibid.

the sake of our integrity. Jesus wants us to take all necessary steps to keep ourselves away from entertaining destructive thoughts. Sin is dangerous and must be dealt with. As such, this resolution must become part of our lives:

For the sake of my integrity, I am willing to be inconvenienced.

Let's look at some practical examples of how this plays out.

I can't tell you how many times I've encouraged someone to install a filter on his computer and he says, "No, it'll only slow it down."

For the sake of my integrity, I am willing to be inconvenienced. I'll install the filter.

A soccer mom has a standing invitation to her girlfriend's house every Friday for wine and cocktails. All her friends attend, and the mom keeps going because she doesn't want to feel left out. Yet, negative and inappropriate things are said and encouraged there. It never goes well for her thought life.

For the sake of my integrity, I am willing to be inconvenienced. I'll skip the party.

A man tells me about the last time he was filled with rage: a driver cut in front of him on the road. He cursed and gave the offending driver an obscene gesture.

For the sake of my integrity, I am willing to be inconvenienced. I'll let him cut ahead.

Take the necessary action. Keep running, even though you're hot, tired, and sweaty. Do whatever it takes to keep yourself free from illicit thoughts. You want the benefit of God's best in all areas—including your thought life.

Third, Fix Your Eyes on Jesus

The final part of Hebrews 12:1–2 directs us to fix our eyes on Christ. This is a positive action, but what does it actually look like to fix our eyes on Jesus? It means we change channels in our mind. We switch off destructive thoughts. We switch on the thoughts of Christ.

Many people are Christians in name only. The idea of fixing their eyes on Christ is completely foreign. Perhaps they consider themselves Christians because they've checked a box on a form because that's what their parents told them when they were young, or because they attend church and celebrate Christmas and Easter. They can begin to fix their eyes on Christ by grasping the foundations of the Gospel: that Jesus saves sinners and makes us new.

How does this one sentence reflect the Gospel? Romans 3:23 declares that we all fall short of the glory of God. Romans 6:23 indicates that because of that sin, we are spiritually separated from God, but Jesus restores the connection. John 3:16 states that belief in Jesus is crucial. Ephesians 2:8–9 clarifies that it's grace that saves us, not works. Second Corinthians 5:17 says, "If anyone is in Christ, the new creation has come: The old has gone, the new is here!" We fix our eyes on Christ whenever we tell ourselves the Gospel.

Yet even after we've grasped the true Gospel, we still might struggle with how to fix our thoughts on Christ throughout a regular day. Perhaps the only thing that comes to mind is that Jesus instructed folks to turn the other cheek. Or perhaps we equate Jesus with a political movement, envisioning a debate. Or we imagine Jesus like He's portrayed in one of those old Sunday school posters—a delicate, blue-eyed Caucasian who walks around cradling a lamb.

That won't cut it. We need to develop, then maintain, a bank of strong mental images of Jesus Christ and His ministry. Then we need to go to those images whenever disappointment arises. We need these images of Christ to be biblically based and not arbitrary so we can fix our thoughts on who He truly is. These mental images are not mere paintings of how artists have imagined Jesus might have looked. Our mental images can display His qualities, characteristics, personality, and attributes. We need to fill our minds with how the Bible presents Him—and then delight in those images. To keep this action memorable, let's use this phrase: "Go to your God-thought." That means we deliberately place into our mind a biblical image of Jesus Christ.

Where might we begin?

Go to Your God-Thought

God-Thought #1:

Jesus creates the universe.

Switch channels to the beginning: Genesis. Does that surprise you? It's easy to think the story of Jesus begins in the manger in Bethlehem. Yet Jesus was active and involved long before His incarnation, when God became flesh and dwelt among us (John 1:14).

We know from Colossians 1:15–16 (NLT) that "Christ existed before anything was created and is supreme over all creation, for through him God created everything.... Everything was created through him and for him." Hebrews 1:2 says, "He [God] has spoken to us by his Son...through whom he made the universe."

I don't pretend to know everything about how this happened. This is intricate theology, but we can't let it scare us away from this amazing truth. Scripture indicates that there is one God (Deuteronomy 6:4), yet He exists in three persons: Father (John 12:28), Son (John 8:58), and Holy Spirit (Acts 13:2). We don't know exactly how the second Person of the Trinity created astrophysics and used it to create the universe, but Scripture says that's what happened. God, through Jesus, created everything. By Jesus, all things were created. All things were created through Jesus.

We can create this mental portrait of Jesus. He was powerful and creative, working before time began. God through Jesus created the heavens and the earth. God through Jesus said, "Let there be light," and there was light. God through Jesus said, "Let there be a sun and a moon," and there was a sun and a moon. God through Jesus created stars and planets and galaxies and solar systems and quasars and black holes and cosmic superclusters. God through Jesus said, "Let there be a man and a woman and let them have minds of their own." God through Jesus declared that all He had created was good. Let's go to our God-thought. Let's fix our minds on that.

God-Thought #2:
Jesus shines brighter than the sun.

Let's create another biblical image to store in our mental banks: Jesus is the transfigured Lord of Glory. Switch channels to that. Matthew 17:1–9 records a powerful story of Jesus taking three of His closest friends—Peter, James, and John—on a hike up a high mountain. There, Jesus's face began to shine like the sun, and His clothes became as white as light. A bright cloud covered them, and a voice from the cloud said, "This is My Son, whom I love; with Him I am well pleased. Listen to Him!" We are called to fix our eyes on this Jesus! He is both "a friend" (John 15:14) and the "Lord of glory" (1 Corinthians 2:7–8), and seeing Him this way can change how we pray.

Have you ever noticed it's easy to be more interested in what we're praying about than Who we are praying to? But when we pray, if we picture this transfigured Lord of Glory, that shifts our priorities. With this mental image of Christ, it's easier to pray: "Lord Jesus, wow—You are incredible. My eyes and thoughts are on You. You are high and lifted up, radiant like the sun. Help me to live for Your name and renown. You are the transfigured Lord, and I want only what you want. Your Kingdom come. Your will be done. My heart is not filled with anxiety about other matters. My eyes are fixed on You."

Let's go to our God-thought. Let's fix our minds on that image of Christ.

God-Thought #3:
Jesus serves us breakfast on the beach.

Let's latch onto another image: Jesus is full of love, grace, and restoration. In the Pattern of Mental Muck, we experience a disappointment or loss, and in our quest for comfort, we turn to that which hinders us and the sins that so easily entangle. Then we're even more miserable. Think about it. If you're disappointed and turn to porn to soothe yourself, you will still be disappointed when you click off the computer—only now, you'll have a host of other lousy feelings, too. Ever been there? You think something like: *Ugh! This again?! What an idiot I am. Surely God is finished with me.* But what if you latched onto a strong mental image of Jesus instead—a restorative image—such as this one?

John 21 records a powerful story about the Apostle Peter.[8] When we first meet him, he's a tough fisherman, full of swagger. Peter follows Jesus for three years and often blows his own horn. He swears he'll be faithful to Christ forever. *Some of those other guys might forsake you, Jesus,* he insists, *but I won't. You can count on me. If you want something done, Jesus, I'm your guy.*

On the night of the last supper, Jesus informs Peter that he will deny Him—and not only once but three times. Peter says it'll never

---

[8] Thanks to Louie Giglio for originally making this passage so clear to us.

happen. But sure enough, soon after Jesus is arrested, Peter lingers in a courtyard. Three times, when asked if he knows Jesus, he says no, he doesn't want anything to do with Him. (Surely that's the essence of sin—both in Peter's life and ours.)

Jesus is crucified. Buried. Raised from the tomb. The walking, talking, breathing Jesus is seen by more than five hundred people (1 Corinthians 15:6). Soon enough, He meets with Peter by the shores of the Sea of Galilee. Peter has returned to fishing by then, convinced he's been canceled.

What happens next in the story is important because it's one of the extremely rare places in Scripture where silence speaks as loudly as words. When the resurrected Jesus meets Peter on the beach, we expect Him to reprimand him. Nobody would fault Jesus for rebuking Peter. But Jesus doesn't have a harsh word for him. He doesn't say to Peter what we expect Jesus to say to us whenever we've blown it: *You are finished. You are worthless. You are canceled.*

There is no accusation.

There is no condemnation.

Instead, Jesus lights a campfire. Switch channels to that. Can you picture yourself there, smelling the wood smoke? The aroma of baking bread wafts up from the fire. Jesus tells Peter and the disciples to bring over some of the fish they've just caught. They're going to have breakfast on the beach.

The conversation that takes place is restorative. Peter is a changed man. He's been humbled by his fall into the Pattern of Mental Muck. Gone now is the swagger and bragging. Instead, Jesus simply asks Peter if he still loves Him. Peter whispers that he certainly does. Jesus reaffirms that Peter has a purposeful mission. He is not finished. Peter is still the beloved child of the Lord of Glory.

And so are we.

Let's go to our God-thought. Let's fix our minds on Christ.

Only the Start

How can we continually fix our thoughts on Christ? Those three images can act as a starting point. Jesus created the universe. Jesus is the transfigured Lord of Glory. Jesus offers us breakfast on the beach. This is the Jesus whom we serve—and this is only the beginning of who Jesus is.

Do we want to be restored today? Here is the new pattern, the new framework that leads to restoration: with Christ's power and our willingness, we throw off the sin that so easily entangles. We don't go to that muck in the first place; instead, we run the race with perseverance, even though the going is hard, and while running, we fix our thoughts on Jesus. We mentally switch channels.

We go to our God-thought.

Create any biblical mental images of Christ you want. Foster your bank of go-to images. Replay them again and again. Are you wondering who Jesus truly is? Open your Bible. You'll see that…

This same Jesus is the Lamb of God who takes away the sin of the world. This same Jesus says, "Come to Me, all you who are weary and burdened, and I will give you rest." This same Jesus is the Bread of Life who sustains and empowers us. This same Jesus is the Light of the World who provides an unobscured path. This same Jesus is the Way, the Truth, and the Life. This same Jesus walks on water and calms the storm. This same Jesus heals the sick and gives sight to the blind. This same Jesus is a friend to sinners. This same Jesus gives hope to the world. This same Jesus feeds the multitudes. This same Jesus says, "I have come to give you abundant life." This same Jesus says, "You can know Me, and you can know My voice." This same Jesus says, "I will go and prepare a place for you, and I will come back again and take you to be with me." This same Jesus says, "When you believe in me, out of your heart will flow rivers of living water." This same Jesus laid down His life that we might live. This same Jesus saves us by His shed blood on the cross. This same Jesus came back to life again. This same Jesus will neither leave us nor forsake us.

This same Jesus sets our minds free.[9]

Key Takeaways

- Disappointment is a part of life, and when we experience loss, naturally, we want to be comforted. Watch out. At that point, we may turn to things that harm our thoughts.
- Instead of turning to harmful thinking, Hebrews 12:1–2 tells us to throw off the sin that so easily entangles us, run with perseverance the race marked out for us, and fix our minds on Christ.
- To fix our eyes on Christ, it's necessary to create a bank of biblical mental images that we can go to whenever we feel disappointed. Then, quickly and effectively, we can "Go to our God-thought."

---

[9] One God-thought is good. Even more God-thoughts are better. Scientists note it's helpful to introduce more than one proactive positive thought to your mind, an idea we flesh out more in Chapter 4. See also Isaac Fradkin and Eran Eldar, "If You Don't Let It In, You Don't Have to Get It Out: Thought Preemption as a Method to Control Unwanted Thoughts," *PLoS Computational Biology* 18, no. 7 (July 13, 2022), https://doi.org/10.1371/journal.pcbi.1010285.

CHAPTER 3

Use Your Real ID

I've had three conversations recently with different people who used the same phrase, or some variation of it. It's one often heard in Christian circles, yet it needs closer examination. Seen in a certain light, or left by itself, it's biblically incomplete—and when wrapped around a Christian's identity, it can hurt people by keeping them bound in the illicitness that enters their thoughts.

The first conversation was with a Christian woman who told me she never looked at pornography, but inside her head were pornographic "home movies" that her imagination produced. She was divorced, and it was not her fault. While she was still married, her husband had drifted into drug use and infidelity and had deserted his family, leaving her and their children bewildered, hurt, and raw. She described how she used sexual fantasies now as a way to escape the pain and abandonment she felt. She felt ashamed about her thought life and wanted to clean out her brain but didn't know what to do. Ultimately, she felt powerless.

"I guess I'm just a divorced woman with a dirty mind," she said with a wry chuckle. "That's the new 'me.' After all, I'm just a sinner saved by grace."

The second person was a friend who sat on my couch and said he needed to talk about something that was plaguing him. He and his wife were in a small group at his church that included a cardiologist, an attorney, the CEO of a successful online pharmaceutical company, and the leading mortgage broker in the area. They were all flush with cash and often talked about the vacations they took, the expensive dinners they had with clients, the new cars they drove, the houses they lived in, and the private colleges their children attended. My friend worked as a contractor and made a family wage, but his take-home pay was nowhere near what the others made.

"I gotta say I'm plain jealous," he said. "Whenever small group is over, my wife and I get in our old truck and drive back to our little split-level. My son is at community college and doing fine, but he wants to go to school out East, which we can't afford. When my family takes vacations, we go to my in-laws' place. Our idea of a fancy dinner out is cheeseburgers and shakes at the drive-through. I know it's wrong to covet your neighbor's stuff, but I can't seem to shake these thoughts. I want what they have, and I find myself angry at them. At my job. At my place in life. Even at God, because He could change things for me if He wanted. The Bible says that envy's a sin, and I know I should just be happy for their success. But I'm not. Thank goodness for grace, because I'm a sinner at my core."

The third person was a man whose wife could do no right. He came for counsel and insisted that his wife disappointed him regularly. He listed several occasions. But the more he talked, I sensed a different narrative emerging. He thought of himself as flawless, while he blamed his wife for every trouble in their marriage—even minor annoyances that sounded to me like the regular stuff of life. If ever they had a difference of opinion, she was always wrong, and he was always right—at least in his eyes.

I asked a few careful questions, and the man sighed and admitted he was stubborn, a bit of a perfectionist, and not particularly empathetic. He had been very close to his mother, a wonderful woman who had died when he was sixteen. He'd made it clear from the start of his marriage that no woman could measure up to his mother's legacy. He confessed that he could be demanding with his friends too, and a few had even confronted him on it.

But he shrugged and added, almost defiantly, "Hey, that's just who I am. A sinner saved by grace. Thank God for 1 John 1:9, because I can't change. Besides, we're here to talk about my wife, right?"

The verse he referenced says, "If we confess our sins, he is faithful and just and will forgive us our sins and purify us from all unrighteousness." The fact that these people have all taken a fearless moral inventory of their lives is good and powerful. That they're seeking help for their thought lives is also good and powerful.

But that's not the problem.

Did you catch the potentially harmful phrase in each of their stories?

"I'm just a sinner saved by grace."

That's the problem.

Tear Up Your Fake ID

The phrase is not wrong, but it is incomplete. It becomes problematic when viewed as our entire identity as Christians. If that is all we believe about ourselves, then we start to think of that as our total identity. Watch out! Because left by itself, it can become a fake ID.

We see TV commercials all the time for identity theft. It's nothing new. Satan has been trying to steal our true identity since the beginning of time. He even uses the Bible—or parts of it—to do so. He tried that tactic with Jesus in the wilderness (see Matthew 4:1–11). But we must not let the devil do that to us anymore. We must understand our fuller identity in Christ, and then live—and think—from that foundation of truth.

What's wrong about merely being "a sinner saved by grace"? Too often it's used as an excuse to keep sinning. A pastor friend is counseling an unmarried Christian couple who are living together. They're constantly saying they're "just sinners saved by grace" instead of dealing with the sin that's besetting them.

When Christians defend this problematic phrase, they point to verses such as Jeremiah 17:9 (KJV), which says, "The heart is deceitful above all things, and desperately wicked: who can know it?" They say, "Look—it's right there in black and white. The Bible says our hearts are deceitful and desperately wicked. That's all we are: sinners, rotten to the core."

But they stopped reading too early. What they don't realize is that the offering of transformed hearts is promised only a few chapters later. In Jeremiah 24:7, God says, "I will give them a heart to know me, that I am the LORD. They will be my people, and I will be their God, for they will return to me with all their heart." In Jeremiah 29:13, God reaffirms this truth: "You will seek me and find me when you seek me with all your heart."

The promises are further reiterated in Ezekiel 11:19 as God says, "I will give them an undivided heart and put a new spirit in them; I will remove from them their heart of stone and give them a heart of flesh." And repeated in Ezekiel 36:26: "I will give you a new heart and put a new spirit in you; I will remove from you your heart of stone and give you a heart of flesh."

The New Testament teaching around the transformation of hearts is likewise full and fantastic. In Romans 2:29, Paul described how, when we are believers, our hearts become "circumcised" by the Holy Spirit. Instead of our bodies literally becoming circumcised with a knife, as the Old Testament folks were commanded to do, our hearts become stripped of sin and spiritually identified with Christ.

Romans 6:1–7 describes how "our self was crucified with him...that we should no longer be slaves to sin." Meaning that our old hearts are indeed desperately wicked and untrustworthy, but our new hearts have the capacity for full spiritual freedom.

One of my favorite verses, 2 Corinthians 5:17, lays this out plainly and wonderfully: "Therefore, if anyone is in Christ, the new creation has come: The old has gone, the new is here!"

This is our new, full identity as believers! Instead of the deceitful and desperately wicked heart ruling our lives, people are offered new hearts that have the capacity to be undivided in pursuing God. The old heart does not need to win any longer!

This truth doesn't eradicate the truth of Romans 3:23—that "all have sinned and fall short of the glory of God." It certainly doesn't change our need for grace in our lives, according to Ephesians 2:8–9: "For it is by grace you have been saved, through faith—and this is not from yourselves, it is the gift of God—not by works, so that no one can boast." But it does make clear our new, core, main identity. In one short, memorable phrase:

I'm a sinner saved by grace who is now a new creation.

Tilt toward the Good

If we constantly identify ourselves by our sin, then it's much easier for us to keep entertaining sin in our minds. *After all, we're just sinners.* But by the power of the Holy Spirit, if we lean toward the "new creation" part of our identity, then we are more apt not to entertain sinful thoughts. Instead, as we seek God from our new hearts and fix our thoughts on Him, our minds are filled with good and noble thoughts.

With our new identity firmly in mind, the action for us to take is to redirect our thoughts away from sin and toward Christ. Pastor John Mark Comer calls the act of thought-redirection "the gift of scripture,"[1] and points believers to the perfect meshing of spiritual practices with modern neuroscience. We don't have to stay stuck in harmful habits of thinking any longer. Neuroscience has shown that we can build new pathways in our brains by thinking helpful things instead of harmful things. The choice is ours. We can redirect our thinking away from the negative and toward the positive. We can choose to dwell on truth. We can enjoy a new quality of life.

Secular psychologist Rick Hanson, Ph.D., invites people toward the simple act of mentally "savoring" good things—his lingo for filling a mind with positive thoughts. He notes it takes only about fifteen to thirty seconds a day to encode a new perspective deep into the fabric of our minds. He writes,

> What do you usually think about at the end of the day? The fifty things that went right, or the one that went wrong? In effect, the brain is like Velcro for negative experiences, but Teflon for positive ones. Besides the

---

[1] John Mark Comer, *Mere Christians* podcast with Jordan Raynor, September 29, 2021, https://podcast.jordanraynor.com/episodes/john-mark-comer-author-of-live-no-lies.

sheer injustice of it, acquiring a big pile of negative experiences in implicit memory banks naturally makes a person more anxious, irritable, and blue. Plus it makes it harder to be patient and giving toward others.

But you don't have to accept this [negativity] bias! By tilting toward the good—"good" in the practical sense of that which brings more happiness to oneself and more helpfulness to others—you level the playing field. In the famous saying, "neurons that fire together, wire together," the more you get your neurons firing about positive facts, the more they'll be wiring up positive neural structures.

Taking in the good is a brain-science savvy and psychologically skillful way to improve how you feel, get things done, and treat others.[2]

I love his phrase, "tilt toward the good." As believers, when we focus on our identity in Christ, the more we wire up positive neural structures in our brains. Reminding ourselves of our identity in Christ is a foundational practice that affects our entire beings for good—what we do, think, and say. When we realize we are sinners saved by grace who are now new creations, and when we choose to daily remind ourselves of this truth—perhaps for as little as fifteen to thirty seconds—our thought lives are gradually and positively affected. The sinful thoughts fall away. The affections of Christ take their place.

With our new identities firmly in mind, whenever we are tempted to sin in our thought life, we can say, "Wait! I am a new

[2] Rick Hanson, "Take in the Good," Rick Hanson, Ph.D, https://www.rickhanson.net/take-in-the-good/; see also Rick Hanson et al., "Learning to Learn from Positive Experiences," *The Journal of Positive Psychology* (December 6, 2021): https://doi.org/10.1080/17439760.2021.2006759.

creation! Wallowing around in sin is not what a new creation does. I'm going to think about something else!"

What Is Our Responsibility?

Sometimes believers fall into another error. We think that because we are new creations, we don't have to deal with sin anymore.

Nothing could be further from the truth. Although it's true that we are new creations, we also bear a responsibility to live out this new-creation life. Remember in the last chapter we discussed Hebrews 12:1-2, noting that sin can still "easily entangle" us? The temptation to sin is still present in a new creation's life, and sin must be dealt with. First John 1:8 says, "If we claim to be without sin, we deceive ourselves and the truth is not in us." This passage is written to believers seeking to live in fellowship with God.

Paul lays out our responsibility in Colossians 3:5-10. We are to "put to death whatever belongs to our earthly nature." And in Ephesians 4:22-24, Paul insists that we must "put off" our old self so we can be "made new in the attitude of our minds." Instead, we must "put on the new self, created to be like God in true righteousness and holiness." This calls for action on our part.

Think of it this way. When we were nonbelievers, we had to sin. We were slaves to sin. But as believers, we have the choice not to sin. Even though sin is prevalent and can easily entangle us, we can prayerfully rid ourselves of it. We can put off our old self and put on our new self.

In Romans 6:1-2 and 11-13, Paul provides a template for living as new creations. He writes:

> What shall we say, then? Shall we go on sinning so that grace may increase? By no means! We are those who

have died to sin; how can we live in it any longer? Count yourselves dead to sin but alive to God in Christ Jesus.

Therefore do not let sin reign in your mortal body so that you obey its evil desires. Do not offer any part of yourself to sin as an instrument of wickedness, but rather offer yourselves to God as those who have been brought from death to life; and offer every part of yourself to him as an instrument of righteousness.

That's how a new creation lives. When tempted, we can use the same phrase as the Apostle Paul: "By no means!" We emphatically don't give in to sin. With all the power that Christ gives us, we prayerfully decide not to let sin rule our life. We don't offer any part of ourselves as instruments of wickedness. Instead, we offer every part of ourselves to God as instruments of righteousness—including our thought life.

Pastor Scott Hubbard writes:

> God wants us to rejoice in the holiness that is already ours in Christ. Our deepest confidence and highest boast before God lie not in our personal holiness, but in the Holy One to whom we are united by faith (1 Corinthians 1:30–31).
>
> If, morning by morning, we breathe in the consolation that comes from being called a saint, then we will run our race with security and joy.[3]

Security, joy, peace—those are just a few of the benefits of not sinning. The moment a harmful thought comes into mind, our call is to rid ourselves of that thought. We replace the sinful thought

---

[3] Scott Hubbard, "Holy Is Who You Are," Desiring God, September 24, 2020, https://www.desiringgod.org/articles/holy-is-who-you-are.

with God's truth. Prayerfully, when any illicit thought comes to mind, we remind ourselves of our true identity. We say: *I don't want this thought. I am a new creation. Holy is who I am.* As such, we are little by little, "transformed by the renewing of our minds" (Romans 12:2).

Your True Name

Have you ever noticed how a person's name affects how they live? This is harder to see if the name is Tom or Betty or Steve. But it's easier to see if the name is "Heel-Grabber" or "Pleasant" or "Servant of an Idol."

"Heel-Grabber" was the name given to the patriarch Jacob. Moments after his twin brother Esau was born, Jacob emerged from his mother's birth canal, still grasping his brother's heel (Genesis 25:26). The name "Jacob" means, literally, "one who follows on another's heels."[4] Figuratively, it means the person is a deceiver.[5]

Jacob's parents weren't being cruel. It was likely a cute-sounding nickname like "Trixie" or "Rascal." Even so, you can envision the danger. If a boy grows up thinking he's a rascal, how might he eventually come to see himself?

Certainly, that's how Jacob lived much of his life. As a youth, the Heel-Grabber tricked Esau into selling his birthright. Jacob deceived his blind, bedridden father into blessing him but not his brother. The man who'd grown up seeing himself as a deceiver used questionable business practices with his uncle Laban to take for himself many of his uncle's flocks and herds.

---

[4] "Jacob" in *Baker's Evangelical Dictionary of Biblical Theology*, ed. Walter A. Elwell (Grand Rapids, Michigan: Baker Book House Company, 1996), https://www.biblestudytools.com/dictionary/jacob/.

[5] Dr. Ralph F. Wilson, "Jacob the Deceiver," JesusWalk Bible Study Series, http://www.jesuswalk.com/jacob/1_deceiver.htm.

Then Jacob's identity was changed. A mysterious person (who many scholars believe was the preincarnate Jesus in bodily form), came into Jacob's life in a big way, wrestling with him for one long night of physical and spiritual struggle (see Genesis 32:22–31). After the wrestling match concluded, Jacob was blessed and given a new name—Israel—which means "God contends," or "Triumphant with God."[6]

The new name reflected a change in identity. Previously, Jacob the Heel-Grabber had lived out of a desperately wicked heart. But with his new identity firmly in place, the man newly named "Triumphant with God" was able to live as a reflection of his empowered relationship with the Lord of Hosts. He didn't become perfect, but he'd reached a watershed moment that changed the direction and outflow of his life.

Incidentally, Israel's hip was dislocated in the wrestling match and he was given a limp. For the rest of his life, his limp reminded him of the power of The Wrestler. Israel needed to consciously depend on the Lord because he needed constant reminding not to think of himself as a deceiver anymore. His call was to live in light of his new changed identity.

During the time of the judges, an Israelite woman named Naomi encountered trouble after trouble—ironic, because her name meant "Pleasant." Famine came to the land of Judah, where Naomi lived with her husband in the town of Bethlehem. To get food, she and her family moved to the idol-worshipping country of Moab. There, her husband died, leaving her with two sons to care for. They grew up and married Moabite women, Ruth and Orpah. Then both of Naomi's sons died. When the famine was over, Naomi and one daughter-in-law, Ruth, returned to Judah,

---

[6] James P. Boyd, *Bible Dictionary* (Baltimore, Maryland: Ottenheimer Publishers, 1958).

while Orpah stayed in Moab. As Naomi and Ruth arrived in Beth-lehem, those who knew her exclaimed, "Can this be Pleasant?!"

"Don't call me Pleasant," Naomi muttered. "Call me Mara (Bitter). I went away full, but the LORD has brought me back empty." (See Ruth 1:19–20.)

Here's some insight into Naomi's efforts to change her name. Never again in the book of Ruth is Naomi referred to as Mara—not by herself, not by others, and certainly not by God. Pleasant is always called Pleasant, a reflection of her invitation to find content-ment in God. Even during hard times, Naomi is encouraged to operate out of her true identity as a sign that God is sovereign over the difficult seasons as well as the good.

Thankfully, much more pleasant things began to happen to Pleasant after she returned to Bethlehem. Her daughter-in-law met and married an upstanding man named Boaz. Through this union, Naomi's lands and wealth were restored. Ruth and Boaz had a son named Obed. In time, he became the grandfather of King David and the direct ancestor of Joseph, the husband of Mary, the mother of Christ (Matthew 1:1–17).

Four highly capable young men named Daniel, Hananiah, Mishael, and Azariah were deported from Israel to Babylon and ordered to serve the idol-worshipping king. All four of their Israelite names reflected the righteous character of God. Daniel means "God is my judge." Hananiah means "God is gracious." Mishael means "Who is like God?" and Azariah means "God has helped."

As part of their indoctrination into the evils of Babylon, the young men were given pagan names that reflected the idolatry of that ancient land. Daniel was renamed Belteshazzar, which meant "Prince of Bel," the name of the main idol of Babylon. Hananiah was renamed Shadrach, which meant "Friend of the King" (of Babylon). Mishael was renamed Meshach, which meant "Worshipper of the idol,

Shach." And Azariah was renamed Abednego, which meant "Servant of the Idol, Nego."[7]

Providentially, the four youths had been rooted in their true identities as servants of the Most High God. Throughout their time in Babylon, they chose not to sin. They stayed true to the Lord as reflections of their original names.

Here's my point. If you call yourself a deceiver, then you'll likely think like a deceiver. If you remind yourself that your name is Pleasant, then you're more prone to stay in that positive perspective when hard times come. If you're a believer and you still think of your sole identity as "sinner," then you're more likely to shrug off the sin in your thought life.

Yet if you know deep within your soul that you are loved and valued by God, then you're more apt to walk in righteousness—even though you might be surrounded by all the evils of a country that's far from God.

Christian, do you know your true name, and are you certain of its potential to affect your life for good?

Your name is New Creation.

Beloved, Holy, Accepted, and More

What does it mean to live as a new creation? Let's look at five specific ways the Bible fleshes out our true identity.

1. We are God's sons and daughters.

First John 3:1 calls us "children of God," and I particularly love how the New Living Translation paraphrases Ephesians 1:5, "God

---

[7] "7 Fascinating Facts That Will Change How You Read the Book of Daniel," *International Bible Society*, October 2, 2018, https://www.biblica.com/articles/7-fascinating-facts-that-will-change-how-you-read-the-book-of-daniel/.

decided in advance to adopt us into his own family by bringing us to himself through Jesus Christ. This is what he wanted to do, and it gave him great pleasure." I have an adopted daughter, and my wife and I take great pleasure in her and all our children. Have you ever thought that God takes "great pleasure" in his relationship with you?

Once, when my adopted daughter was young, we were set to go for a bike ride. She took off ahead of me, but unfortunately, we were on a slight incline and she was still getting used to working the brakes. If she didn't stop quickly, she was going to smack straight into a huge steel garbage bin.

I dropped my bike and sprinted after her. Just before she hit, I dove headfirst like a runner sliding into home plate. I grabbed my daughter and held on tight. She missed the bin, but I wasn't so lucky. I hit the pavement, ground to a halt, and came up bloodied.

Funny: afterward, I was grinning. I wasn't thinking of my pain. I was thinking only of my beloved daughter. The incident gave me perspective into how Jesus could suffer and die on a cross because He loves us. When I was diving for my daughter, I set aside what happened to me. My goal was to save her. Jesus took Hell on the cross for us. He was willing to go through infinite suffering and pain for His adopted children.

2. We are Jesus's friends.

In John 15:15, Jesus calls us His "friends." Have you ever considered yourself a friend of Christ? I was raised on that great old hymn, "What a Friend We Have in Jesus." But for years, I didn't think of Jesus as a friend. I knew He had died for me. I had accepted Him as my savior. I was following Him. Yet due to the sins that still entangled my life, I'd concluded He wasn't very happy with me.

Here's the truth: our sins are forgiven (Ephesians 1:7). Grace abounds (Romans 5:20). The Bible calls Jesus our friend.

3. We are rescued from darkness.

Colossians 1:13–14 describes how God "has rescued us from the dominion of darkness and brought us into the kingdom of the Son he loves."

I remember seeing in the news how rain pummeled Washington state some time back. The dirt became mud, a hillside gave way, and some people became trapped in the muddy slide. They struggled to get free, but they were too mired to be rescued. Tragically, they died.

Sometimes we can feel like we're too deeply mired to be rescued. We live like we're stuck in the mud, inches away from death. But God's rescue is all-powerful. We cannot sink so far into our sins that we cannot be rescued by Jesus. The main rescue has already happened. He brought us from darkness to light. As we remind ourselves of that truth, we find ourselves becoming unstuck.

4. We are accepted in Christ.

Romans 15:7 describes how Christ has "accepted" us. I love that word; it's one of the most powerful in the English language.

We might be judged or rejected by others, but we are accepted by Christ. We might be abandoned by friends or family, but we are accepted by Christ. We might be forgotten or forsaken or slighted or scorned by people, but we are accepted by Christ.

How does this acceptance occur? Through the work Christ did on the cross. God so loved the world that He sent Jesus to take the penalty of sin for us. God's love doesn't stop there. God loves us always and fully. Nothing can separate us from the love of God (see Romans 8:38–39).

When we understand what Christ has done for us, how His love never fails, and how His acceptance forms a big piece of our identity, then we are more prone to avoid sin. We don't need to turn to illicit thoughts to feel better. We can turn to the Person who's already accepted us.

5. We are chosen, royal, and holy.

In 1 Peter 2:9, the apostle notes that we are chosen, royal, and holy. These are words that show value, distinction, and cleanness. This is the way God sees us. This is our true identity.

"New Creation" Thought Life

Let's draw some conclusions about how new-creation living affects our everyday life. Remember those three people who began the chapter? Here's what we could say to encourage them:

You are not "a divorced woman with a dirty mind." That's a fake identity. Do not tell yourself that any longer. Yes, the truth of your life is that your husband left you and you were hurt. But equally true is that God accepts you; He has not forsaken you. You are His beloved daughter, and He has chosen and transformed you into holy royalty. That is who you are at the core. You don't need to fill your mind with illicit thoughts. They won't help you. Each day, for a minimum of fifteen seconds, remind yourself of your new identity. You are a new creation. The old has gone. The new has arrived.

Let your thinking flow from your true identity.

You who are plagued by jealousy: you are not merely a sinner saved by grace. That's an incomplete identification. Do not tell yourself that any longer. Yes, the truth is that you are attracted to what your friends have, and you're envious that you don't have the same things. But equally true is that God has forgiven you and rescued you from the dominion of darkness and brought you into the Kingdom of the Son He loves. You are no longer a slave to sin. You are God's beloved child, and you are holy royalty. That is who you are. You don't need to fill your mind with thoughts of what you don't have. Those thoughts won't help you. Maybe you'll need to switch small groups, but perhaps you can begin to see the people in your small group as having their own troubles, and you'll begin to pray for them. No one's life is perfect, and nobody's life is free from harm. In the meantime, each day, for a minimum of fifteen seconds, remind yourself of your new identity. You are a new creation. The old has gone. The new has arrived.

Let your thinking flow from your true identity.

Dear stubborn Christian, you are not bound by your perfectionism. Undoubtedly you are still grieving the loss of your mother, who meant much to you. But you can't take out your grief on your spouse or friends. Jesus understands everything there is to know about your life, and He gives you the grace for contentment and the power to change. The annoyances you feel toward your spouse do not need to be part of your life any longer. She is not "wrong," and you are not "right." You are different from each other, and God created you to have distinct perspectives. Your marriage is actually stronger because of this. So, you can throw those old thoughts away. Instead, ask the Lord to fill your mind with the affections of Christ. Pray that God would give you a new and considerate love for your spouse. You are a holy and beloved adopted child of God—and so is she. Each day, for a minimum of fifteen seconds, remind yourself of your new identity. You are a new creation. The old has gone. The new has arrived.

The truth sets us free. May we all let our thinking flow from our new identity in Christ.

Key Takeaways

- The oft-heard phrase "I'm just a sinner saved by grace" is problematic when left as is. It can be used as an excuse to keep sinning. As believers, if we think of ourselves only or primarily as sinners, then we're more apt to live as sinners and entertain sinful thoughts.
- The Bible indicates we are new creations. The old has gone, the new has arrived. This is our true identity. Our responsibility is to throw off sin and prayerfully live as a reflection of our new identity.
- As new creations, we are loved by God, accepted by God, friends of Christ, forgiven, rescued, chosen, royal, and holy. As we let our thinking flow from our true identity, we exchange sinful thoughts for thoughts that align with the affections of Christ.

CHAPTER 4

Purple Elephant, Orange Monkey

H ere's a fun mental exercise—and it has a larger point that goes beyond fun, I promise. For the next fifteen seconds while you're reading, I want you not to think about a big purple elephant. The key is "not." Just get that big purple elephant right out of your head. We'll keep track of the seconds informally using the "Mississippi" technique. The clock starts now.

One Mississippi. Do not imagine a big purple elephant. *Two Mississippi.* Do not picture a long, purplish trunk on the front of your elephant. *Three Mississippi.* Don't envision two flappy violet-colored elephant ears on the sides of his head. *Four Mississippi.* Don't imagine two splendid plum-colored ivory elephant tusks. *Five Mississippi.* Whatever you do, don't visualize that thick, saggy-baggy, pomegranate-colored skin that covers your purple elephant. *Six Mississippi.* Get that purple pachyderm out of your head right now. *Seven Mississippi.* There is absolutely no purple elephant in your mind. *Eight Mississippi...*

Time out! We'll press pause on the clock for a moment. How's it going? Are you *not* thinking about your purple elephant?

Okay, let's move to the next part of the game. What I want you to do now is envision a gigantic, orange, talking monkey riding a motorcycle. Can you picture that crazy image in your mind? The monkey is orange, remember. He's going to say something in a moment, because this monkey talks. And we have to wonder where he'll ride off to on his motorcycle. The fifteen-second clock will start up again from where we last left off. Go!

Nine Mississippi. Picture your orange monkey's beady apricot-colored eyes. *Ten Mississippi.* Imagine that monkey's furry cantaloupe-colored belly. *Eleven Mississippi.* See in your mind's eye your monkey's curly carrot-colored tail. *Twelve Mississippi.* Hey ho! That orange monkey kickstarts his Harley-Davidson and rip-roars like a rocket in an astonishing vertical line straight up the side of a tree. *Thirteen Mississippi.* He ditches his motorcycle on the top branch and leaps into the air. *Fourteen Mississippi.* He catches a vine with both hands, swings through the jungle foliage, and calls out with a voice clear and keen: "Ooh-ooh-ah-ah! I'm going bananas!"

Fifteen Mississippi. Time's up. Congratulations. You know what just happened?

You stopped thinking about your purple elephant.

The Strength of an Exchange

Scottish theologian Thomas Chalmers (1780–1847) preached a sermon that became famous in its era entitled "The Expulsive Power of a New Affection." Consider the importance of each main word in that title. *Expulsive* means something is discharged or ejected, forced out with intensity. An *affection*, in this case, is something for which we have a fond attachment. It's what we desire. Chalmers's sermon was later turned into a booklet and widely circulated. The reading itself can be demanding because he uses a lot of archaic words, yet his thesis is clear from the title. Do we want to get rid of sinful thoughts? Good. Then we need to put God-honoring thoughts in their place. A new affection contains expulsive power.

Chalmers based much of his message on 1 John 2:15: "Do not love the world or anything in the world. If anyone loves the world, love for the Father is not in them." He reasoned that the human heart must exchange the love of the world for godly affections. If we merely try to do away with sinful affections, then once they're gone, a void or vacuum is left and it must be filled. Consequently, he writes,

> We know of no other way by which to keep the love of the world out of our hearts than to keep in our hearts the love of God. This is not a duty one performs. It is a delight one prefers.[1]

This is the important transaction for us to note: We get rid of the love of the world by filling our hearts with the love of God.

The swap is vital. One thought must be exchanged for another. If all we're trying to do is not think a thought, then it's quite difficult to effectively jettison that thought. We can grit our teeth and try with all our might not to think about a purple elephant. But if our only efforts are undertaken toward removal, then getting rid

---

[1] Thomas Chalmers, *The Expulsive Power of a New Affection* (Wheaton, Illinois: Crossway Short Classics, 2020), 16.

of that thought is quite hard to do, particularly if we're reminding ourselves of that specific thought. *Don't think about the purple elephant! Don't think about the purple elephant!* Instead, we must put a different thought in its place. When we thought of a gigantic orange monkey riding a motorcycle up the side of a tree, it was much easier to forget the purple elephant. The second thought pushed out the first.

Chalmers wrote,

> The [sinful] habit cannot so be replaced as to leave nothing but a negative and cheerless vacancy behind it. The ascendant power of a second affection will do what no exposition, however forcible, of the folly and worth-lessness of the first ever could effectuate. We have to address to the eye of [the] mind another object, with a charm powerful enough to dispossess the first of its influences. The throne must have an occupier.[2]

The action of exchanging thoughts is similar to the one we discussed in Chapter Two, "Go to Your God-Thought," but the replacement of affections is more involved because we don't merely provide for ourselves one quick thought or image. Instead, we develop a lifestyle in which we relentlessly cultivate powerful and alluring godly thoughts. Our mind becomes a true seedbed of positive affections that continually grow and flourish. In practical terms, this is what is instructed in Colossians 3:2, "Set your mind on things above," and in Hebrews 3:1–3, "Fix your thoughts on Jesus."

Ultimately, we find freedom, peace, confidence, and self-respect when we do this, because we consistently encounter the power and

---

[2] Ibid., 33, 47.

kindness of a transcendent and immanent God, as well as the beauty, excellence, and nobility of all things that align with His heart. We are not merely trying to remove a harmful thought from our mind. We are prayerfully aiming, with God's help, to fill our mind—and all our life—with Him, including "every good and perfect gift" that He offers (James 1:17).

A Superior Pleasure

Modern-day theologian John Piper, commenting on Chalmers's sermon, wrote:

> The most effective way to kill our own sin is by the power of a superior pleasure. No one sins out of duty. We sin because it [seems] more pleasant or less painful than the way of righteousness. So, bondage to sin is broken by a stronger attraction—a more compelling joy.[3]

People don't turn to pornography or pornographic thoughts because they're obligated to do so. No one starts a week by saying, "Okay, I need to work forty hours this week because my boss expects me to. I need to volunteer at my kids' school because I'm obliged to help out. I'm required to show up at the courthouse for jury duty on Friday because I got a summons in the mail to be a juror—so I've got a legal duty there. And, oh yeah, I must stare at porn at least an hour every night because I'm *required* to do so."

In some cases, an addiction might be present when a person watches pornography, so we could argue that an addicted person

---

[3] John Piper, "'The Expulsive Power of a New Affection'": The Life-Changing Insight of Thomas Chalmers," Desiring God, October 23, 2019, https://www.desiringgod.org/articles/the-expulsive-power-of-a-new-affection.

feels a compulsive pull toward porn. But a compulsion is different than a legal, vocational, or spiritual obligation. As believers, we have no duty to sin—and amen to that! The removal of our obligations to sin is what we discussed in depth last chapter. Romans 6:6 indicates that we are "no longer slaves to sin."

Instead, the reason that we sometimes choose to succumb to sin, in Piper's words, is because sin seems "more pleasant or less painful than the way of righteousness." This gets to the heart of the Pattern of Mental Muck discussed in Chapter Two. Something negative happens to us, and that prompts us to feel disappointment. So we naturally seek comfort, soothing, or relief. We swallow the fake fact that it will feel more pleasant or less painful to turn toward an illicit thought than anything else. Thus, we make our choice and indulge in sin.

What's the solution? We must replace the sin with a superior pleasure. We don't merely try to stop thinking illicit thoughts. If our only efforts are put toward stopping something or getting rid of something, then that's mentally quite difficult. We wind up constantly thinking, *I can't think about junk! I must stop thinking about junk! I have to get these images out of my head!* In effect, we become fixated on the trouble, which keeps our mind engaged on it. Typically, all this does is induce anxiety in us. It whips us into a frenzy of trying to remove sin.

Have you ever had a catchy commercial jingle stuck in your head? Maybe the same commercial played five times during a single TV show. The show finished, but that song kept running through your mind until you became sick of it. You might not have even liked the product being advertised. But all night long your mind mentally replayed that same jaunty ditty.

The jingle might fade from your mind on its own in time, but the surest way to get rid of one stuck song is to turn on a different tune and get different music playing through your mind. You replace one song with the other.

It works the same way with any mentally stuck thought. The solution is to exchange the harmful for the helpful. Instead of feeling fear, we remind ourselves of our security in Christ. Instead of replaying an envious thought in our minds, we remind ourselves that "godliness with contentment is great gain" (1 Timothy 6:6). Instead of feeling rage, we pray for calmness and understanding. Instead of holding grudges, we pray to see people with eyes of compassion. We replace the God-dishonoring with the God-honoring.

Captive! Get Out, in Jesus's Name!

From a biblical perspective, the encouragement to exchange thoughts is found in Scripture, but we need to look closely to see it. Consider how all of Scripture works in harmony with itself. People can get into trouble when they lift one verse out of context and look only at it. Conversely, a biblical truth can be correctly augmented or expanded upon by looking at more than one verse on the subject at a time.

Remember how we discussed what Satan did with Jesus during His time of testing? In Matthew 4:6, Satan led Jesus to the roof of the temple then used a snippet of Scripture lifted from its context to tempt Him. "If you are the Son of God," the devil said, "throw yourself down. For it is written: 'He will command his angels concerning you, and they will lift you up in their hands, so that you will not strike your foot against a stone.'" The devil was quoting Psalm 91:11–12. Jesus responded in a fuller context by quoting Deuteronomy 6:16: "It is also written, 'Do not put the LORD your God to the test.'"

I find it fascinating that Jesus not only responded to temptation with Scripture, but He chose a verse that wasn't in close proximity to the one that Satan quoted. Jesus's verse isn't found in the same chapter, or even in the same book. In Jesus's time, the Old Testament was grouped into a three-fold division: the Law of Moses, the Prophets, and the Writings, which included the Psalms. The devil quoted a verse from the third section of the canon, the Psalms. Jesus responded with a verse from the first section, the Law. That's fine, because the fullest context of scripture is all of Scripture. All of Scripture agrees with itself.

The concept of exchanging one thought for another is found in at least two separated verses, both written by the Apostle Paul under the inspiration of the Holy Spirit. Getting rid of illicit thoughts is found in 2 Corinthians 10:5b. Filling our mind with godly thoughts is found in Philippians 4:8 (and many other verses). What we need to grasp is that it's more effective to live out the instructions of 2 Corinthians 10:5b when we link that verse with the instructions in Philippians 4:8. Let me explain.

Second Corinthians 10:5b is extremely powerful: "We take captive every thought to make it obedient to Christ." Paul is appealing to fellow believers to wage spiritual battles the most effective way. Harmful thoughts lead to harmful living, he's saying. Those harmful thoughts must be captured like they're criminals. He urges believers to grab anything that's false or damaging or holds a believer in bondage—grab it for the purpose of dealing with it in light of Christ's truth. He instructs believers to take captive every illicit thought.

What might it look like to take a thought captive? The Greek word for "take captive" is *aichmalōtizō*. It's the same word translated in Luke 24:24 as "taken as prisoners" and in 2 Timothy 3:6

as "gain control." It's judicial language. Rebellious thoughts must be seized, arrested, and locked up or done away with. It's also military language. When a battle is waged and enemy soldiers are captured, the prisoners of war are rounded up and deported to another land. Similarly, any and every illicit thought that enters our mind must be seized like a captured enemy, placed under the full authority of Jesus, and ultimately removed from our presence.

Practically, this removal is empowered by prayer. I asked a wise friend how he does this, and he said that whenever an illicit thought enters his mind, he immediately thinks in prayer: "Captive! Get out, in Jesus's name!" Literally, he says those words in his mind. The illicit thought doesn't have any time to worm its way into his mind where it can be entertained. I like that approach very much.

Still, when an illicit thought is taken captive and removed, a void can be left. This is where we need the expulsive power of a new affection. It's hard to push an illicit thought out of our mind without replacing it with a better thought. It's also difficult to keep an illicit thought out for the long term without putting a God-honoring thought in its place. In Piper's teaching, we need "a superior pleasure." We need the injection of a thought more pleasant than the illicit thought. We need to fill our minds with the stronger attraction, the more compelling joy.

That's where Philippians 4:8 goes hand-in-hand with 2 Corinthians 10:5. Once an illicit thought is taken captive and pushed aside in prayer, we can fill our minds with Christ-honoring thoughts. Or, seen in reverse: we can remove illicit thoughts by thinking Christ-honoring thoughts. Philippians 4:8 says, "Finally, brothers and sisters, whatever is true, whatever is noble, whatever is right, whatever is pure, whatever is lovely, whatever is admirable—if anything is excellent or praiseworthy—think about such things."

The instruction in Philippians 4:8 is given in an immediate context of joy. Paul encourages believers to rejoice in a spirit of gentleness because the Lord is near. He encourages us not to be anxious about anything, but to pray instead, presenting all requests to God. Peace and confidence comes to us then, with Christ's help, as we fill our minds with good things. We can experience a new quality of life.

Seen in the context of overturning the Pattern of Mental Muck, the sequence looks like this: Something negative happens to us. That causes us to feel disappointment. We naturally seek comfort, soothing, or relief. We are tempted to believe the lie that it will feel more pleasant or less painful to turn toward sin. But instead, we can immediately take that thought captive. We don't have to indulge in sin. We pray in our mind, "Captive! Get out, in Jesus's name!" Then we deliberately go to our God-thought, the mental image of Christ that we've previously created and can quickly access. Or—and this is where Philippians 4:8 becomes so powerful and even fun—we can mentally turn to any true and noble thought that honors God.

Because an important word in Philippians 4:8 is "whatever." It's used six times in that one verse. The Greek word for whatever is *hosos*. It's a qualifying word that means "as many as." Meaning: many things are true—so think about as many truths as you wish. Many things are noble—so think about as many of those things as you want. And so on. It's a wonderfully liberating verse that invites us to feast at a smorgasbord of God-honoring goodness.

May this become our new habit! May we take captive every sinful thought and fill our minds instead with God-honoring and truly compelling joys.

Cue, Routine, Reward

A Pulitzer Prize-winning journalist named Charles Duhigg wrote an insightful book called *The Power of Habit* that spent more than three years on the *New York Times* bestsellers list. The entire book is helpful and recommended. If you're looking for a condensed version of his process and thesis, it's this: Duhigg studied the research of leading psychologists, sociologists, and neuroscientists, synthesized their findings, and concluded essentially the same things as Chalmers, Piper, and the Apostle Paul. Namely, it's quite hard to get rid of a bad habit, such as smoking, if all you do is try to remove it. Instead, you must replace the harmful habit with a helpful one, such as going for a walk. When a new affection comes into a person's life, it enters with expulsive power.

Duhigg described the neuroscience of making and breaking habits. It corresponds with Scripture, although he doesn't use the same terminology. We can break a harmful habit by taking every thought captive. We can make a helpful habit by consistently focusing on that which is truthful, right, pure, lovely, admirable, excellent, or praiseworthy. The secret to breaking any harmful habit is to create a new and helpful habit, and then to convince the brain to enjoy the helpful habit by pairing it with a reward that's genuinely pleasurable. We must seek and entertain a more compelling joy.

In Duhigg's terminology, every habit has three components: a cue, a routine, and a reward. Brains light up the most during the first and third components of the loop—the cue and the reward. During the mid-part of the loop—the routine—the brain functions almost on autopilot. For years, when people tried to break habits, they focused solely on the routine, but that didn't work very effectively. The routine is the overtly behavioral part of the habit loop—the smoking, the sugary soda consumption, the mental replaying of illicit thoughts. When people tried only to alter the routine, the harmful habits didn't break but persisted as strongly as ever. But when people examined and altered the cue and reward, then harmful habits were broken and replaced.

For example, a group of German researchers wanted to help sedentary people exercise. They gathered some seven hundred people and split them into two groups. The first group was simply instructed to exercise. The second group was instructed to create a cue, such as placing their exercise clothes next to their bed, so they would notice their workout clothes each morning and remind themselves to go running. They were also told to create a reward, such as eating a tiny piece of chocolate at the end of each run. The results? Those who had established and defined a cue and a reward habitually exercised twice as much as the other group.[4]

If we want to break a harmful habit, we need to incentivize ourselves toward the helpful. It's much harder to motivate ourselves if all we're trying to do is avoid a harm. Marketers discovered this several years ago with a chemical first known by its technical term, "HPBCD." The chemical didn't simply mask a bad odor. It removed a bad odor entirely. Marketers named it Febreze, and they started running commercials saying that Febreze would get rid of all the bad smells on any piece of fabric. A doggy smell on a couch would disappear. The cigarette smell on a smoker's clothes would evaporate. The stinky shoe smell on a carpet would vanish.

But Febreze didn't sell. Marketers wondered why and went back to the drawing board. They discovered that people who live

---

[4] Google Zeitgeist, "How Do Habits Work? | Charles Duhigg | Google Zeitgeist," YouTube, October 16, 2012, https://www.youtube.com/watch?v=AOPICbCxaFA.

with bad smells gradually become desensitized to the odors. They aren't as concerned about ridding themselves of bad smells because the smells no longer greatly affect them. The problem doesn't feel like a problem.

It was an age-old truth they discovered, but it took a while to see. People are more motivated by incentives than deterrents. The dangling carrot in front of an ox's nose is more effective than the whip on its back. So the marketers changed their ad campaigns to encourage people to use Febreze as a reward at the conclusion of their cleaning—so a home would smell as good as it looked. The stated reward for using Febreze was not to get rid of the bad, but to usher in and promote the good. The result? Bottles of Febreze started flying off the shelves, soon joining the parent company's $1 Billion Club.[5] That's a *billion* dollars in sales each year—just from Febreze.

It's important to grasp this truth on a spiritual plane. The building of helpful mental habits is an integral and necessary part of eradicating harmful mental habits. Let's say we're currently stuck in a harmful habit of thinking the same illicit thought over and over again. Perhaps each time we go to bed at night, we fill our mind with images of people we used to date and the premarital physical intimacy we might have experienced. If our contact was limited, we might extrapolate scenarios and imagine a furtherance of physical contact between us and an ex. Those replayed images feel comforting to us. Our day has been hard, or maybe we haven't gotten along with our spouse, so the illicit sexual images feel familiar and reassuring. We remember only the thrills of the bygone relationships but not the lows. The illicit thoughts prompt us to forget the trouble of our day. The sin puts us to sleep.

[5] Ellen Byron, "Febreze Joins P&G's $1 Billion Club," *Wall Street Journal*, March 9, 2011, https://www.wsj.com/articles/SB10001424052748704076804576180683371307932.

Yet in our clearest moments, we're alarmed by this habit. We know we're dishonoring our spouse by imagining someone else. The earlier intimate relationships were not God-honoring. Replaying or extrapolating those thoughts is ultimately sinful. We want to change this habit. But if all we try to do is remove the illicit thoughts from our mind, then it's an uphill battle. The key is to examine the cue—every time we lay our head down, we start having illicit thoughts. And then shift the reward—being soothed to sleep. Then we can prayerfully change our routine.

What if, instead of imagining an ex, we imagined a soothing river instead. We like fly-fishing. That's a true joy for us. The imagined river flows without interruption, and it's cheerfully bubbling, filled with fish. There's no drama with the river. No confrontations, arguments, tension, or breakups. None of the things that actually happened with our exes. Our fly rod swishes back and forth above the waters. It's a God-honoring mental image. God made rivers. God made fish. Rivers and fish are good.

The cue is still there—when we lie down, we fill our mind with a thought. But the thought that's associated with the cue has been shifted. Instead of being lulled to sleep by a sinful fantasy, we now drift off to sleep with the God-honoring image of fly-fishing. Similarly, the reward is different. The real reward is the peace we feel the next morning. When we awake, we know in our heart we didn't sin the night before. Thanks to the cue being acknowledged and the reward being shifted, our routine starts to change. We've prayerfully taken an illicit thought captive, and we've replaced it with something that's true and right and noble and lovely. Ultimately, we have fixed our mind on a more compelling joy.[6]

---

[6] For a summary of the teachings of Duhigg's book, see Art of Manliness, "The Power of Habit | Art of Manliness," YouTube, June 23, 2013, https://www.youtube.com/watch?v=7vubNNfhSvc&t=160s.

Your Redeemed Imagination

As Christians, we can get fixated on negative thoughts quite easily. It doesn't matter if the negative thought is about a relationship gone wrong or something generated by the six o'clock news. We correctly want to stand up for truth, so we mistakenly believe the best way of doing that is railing against the negative.

It's true—1 Thessalonians 5:22 instructs us to "reject every kind of evil." Yet a huge and important part of the Christian life is to steer clear of the negatives and instead fix our thoughts on the positives—even to *imagine* new positives. Toward this endeavor, it's vitally important not to gloss over the teaching of Philippians 4:8 and other verses. We don't want to rattle off virtues merely like items on a grocery list: true, noble, right, pure, lovely, admirable, excellent, praiseworthy. *Got it!*

My encouragement is to regularly take time to define and articulate what each of those virtues in Philippians 4:8 looks like for you. Create extended, expansive definitions of these virtues, then fill your mind with those thoughts. Perhaps the ideas below will spur you onward.

- True: Think of things that line up with reality, that gibe with what actually exists. You know how you get a subliminal pleasure in seeing pictures hanging straight on a wall? Like that, there is healing in seeing truth as true. Ultimately, we have Jesus's statement, "I am the Truth" (John 14:6). Stir that around in your brain for a while.
- Noble: What calls for our respect today? Mull that over. The noble, the ethical, the moral—fill your mind with these thoughts.

- Right: Well, that's the opposite of wrong. Think about things that are correct and that line up with what's holy, good, and good for you.
- Pure: These are things unmixed with contaminates, everything from a glass of fresh-squeezed lemonade to unmixed motives and honest statements, to a husband and wife deeply in love without the contamination of straying extramarital thoughts.
- Lovely: Just look around you. "Lovely" isn't a word we use every day, but loveliness abounds—a wisp of cloud catching the sun, a half-faded flower, a well-shaped rock, a baby's cheeks, a loaf of fresh bread perfectly crusted, a friend who asks, "How are you doing?" Ponder those things.
- Admirable: What things are to be admired? In this category are things that earn a good reputation because they are moral, noble, right, ethical—and the thought circles right back to true and honorable.
- Excellent: These are the things that rise above mediocrity. A well-crafted song. A finely built automobile. The running and tackling abilities of a focused and highly trained athlete.
- Praiseworthy: What prompts you to cheer? What things are commendable and laudable?

God does not call us simply to eradicate harmful fantasies. He has given us minds capable of rich imagination. We can become mentally inventive as an expression of being made in the image of God (Genesis 1:27). Have you ever considered that when God created the heavens and the earth, He first imagined what it was all going to be like? All of His creation sprang from the holy, wonderful, and infinitely inventive mind of God.

He has called us to fill our minds with holy, wonderful, and infinitely imaginative thoughts. We are called to think using the fullest capacities of our minds—deep thoughts, beautiful thoughts, noble thoughts, incredibly creative and wondrous thoughts. When we dwell upon sinful thoughts, they distort our imagination. But when we fill our minds with thoughts of God and the abundance of images that honor Him—and act on those thoughts—then we are truly living to please Him (2 Corinthians 5:9).

As internationally renowned Christian artist Makoto Fujimura writes,

> The God of the Bible is the God of abundance. Therefore, Jesus' preaching addresses the mindsets of scarcity-ridden, fear-filled followers. "Consider the lilies," "love your enemies," "blessed are the poor," the many parables that assume abundance at the core of our lives—they all point to the greater love.
>
> When we say God is purposeful, we need to move beyond our industrial mindset of bottom-line thinking about efficiency and success. God is gratuitously purposeful to bring vast, abundant beauty into our lives.
>
> God did not build us as survival machines that would function like clockwork; we are creatures of magnificence and imagination, made in the image of God. We are not like horses that are being trained to jump higher and higher. Instead, we are, as C. S. Lewis puts it, horses that have grown wings.[7]

---

[7] Makoto Fujimura, *Art and Faith* (New Haven, Connecticut: Yale University Press, 2020), 78–9.

Think about how the God-honoring imaginations of Christians have been positively expressed throughout history.[8]

In the third century AD, believers in Jesus Christ painted beautiful frescoes on the Roman catacombs, even in an era when Christians were under attack.

The haunting, melodic sounds of Gregorian chants were originally created in the sixth century AD, helping to quiet the minds of the hearers and express their worship of God.

The windows of the Sainte-Chapelle chapel in Paris are filled with intricate stained glass, and the building was consecrated in AD 1248. Dazzling images of the entire progress of redemption—from Adam and Eve to Revelation—appear in those windows. Worshippers find themselves breathless at the sight.

The paintings of Caravaggio and Albrecht Dürer, the sonnets of John Donne and the poems of T. S. Eliot, the symphonies of Mendelssohn and Bach, the elaborate plot structure and characters in J. R. R. Tolkien's *The Lord of the Rings*—all these imaginative expressions of faith sprang from minds entwined with the creativity of God. The artisans themselves weren't perfect, yet they all allowed their minds to bask in rich, God-honoring ingenuity.

Wonder awaits you. Allow the Lord of Hosts to fill your mind with His goodness. Choose to fix your mind on whatever is God-honoring, true, noble, right, pure, lovely, admirable, excellent, and praiseworthy. Then act upon your thoughts, and see what God does through your mind when it's focused on Christ and filled with the Holy Spirit. What kind of masterpieces—big or small, famous or obscure, permeated with talent or simple, raw, and free—will God create through you?

---

[8] For a helpful book on this subject, see Terry Glaspey, *75 Masterpieces Every Christian Should Know: The Fascinating Stories behind Great Works of Art, Literature, Music, and Film* (Chicago: Moody Publishers, 2015).

Key Takeaways

- One of the most effective ways to stop thinking an illicit thought is to start thinking a God-honoring thought. The positive thought pushes the illicit thought away and fills our minds with something good.
- In practical spiritual living, 2 Corinthians 10:5b and Philippians 4:8 work best in tandem. We prayerfully take an illicit thought captive. And we think about whatever is true, noble, right, pure, lovely, admirable, excellent, or praiseworthy. The two actions can happen almost simultaneously.
- God has called us to fill our minds with holy, wonderful, and infinitely imaginative thoughts. God has given us minds and hearts capable of rich imagination, and believers are called to think using the fullest capacities of creativity.

CHAPTER 5

Check under the Hood

Imagine you're at your doctor's office. She asks, "What's wrong?"

"Well, Doctor," you say, "I have a persistent fever. I'm tired all the time. And I'm rapidly losing weight without trying."

"No problem," she says. "Use some over-the-counter pain reliever to bring down that fever. Buy a new pillow so you can sleep better at night. Try harder to eat more at mealtimes. We'll have you fixed up in no time." She pats you on the back, points you to the door, and sends you the bill.

What went wrong during that encounter?

On a surface level, all the advice sounds helpful. A pain reliever can reduce fever. A new pillow might help a person sleep better. Food is important for an empty stomach. But the doctor failed to ask one extremely important question. Do you know what it was?

What's causing these symptoms?

The doctor is treating only what she immediately sees. In doing so, she's glossing over the core problem. She's failing to look beneath the symptoms so she can discover the underlying cause. The persistent fever, chronic tiredness, and inexplicable weight loss are being produced by something that's gone wrong inside the body. That's what needs to be treated. Perhaps the root cause is the flu, tuberculosis, hepatitis, or even leukemia. There is a greater reason why this patient is sick, but the doctor is failing to search for the fuller cause.

A similar thing happens on a spiritual level. A person might come to me and say, "Steve, I'm looking at porn every night. I'm frustrated all the time, and almost any minor irritation seems to trigger a burst of rage. I'm nervous a lot—waves of anxiety constantly wash over me. What should I do?"

We can start by treating symptoms. That's not wrong. Sometimes an overt ailment needs to be addressed immediately to bring calm, safety, or stability to a person or their family. In some situations, I'll suggest ways a person can minimize the chances of being triggered in the first place. If symptoms are so overwhelming as to cause self-destructive tendencies or potential harm to others, I'll recommend psychiatric evaluation to determine if an effective medication can help.

Yet in due course, I want to dig down and understand the root cause of the symptoms. The root cause needs to be healed by Christ so the person can move forward in health. Something in the heart of the person is causing these destructive behaviors and thoughts. Somewhere along the line, this person has been hurt, abandoned, saddened, or maligned. At their core level, they are grappling with a deeper kind of chaos.

Bible teacher Jon Snyder writes:

> Lust and fantasy are always symptoms of a deeper problem. The Bible says that out of the heart flow the issues we face, not the other way around. Sin is the manifestation of something out of order at a much deeper level.

This is why we often fight against lust without seeming to win the war. Then when we see the problem resurface, we feel as though the rug has been pulled out from under us and face discouragement and hopelessness.

Until we deal with the root, sin functions in our hearts a lot like weeds growing in a garden. You pull the weed and think, "That's the end of that. I got it this time!" Only, it comes back again and again. So what does a wise gardener do? He [deals with] the root.[1]

If we can understand what it is inside us that's been hurt, damaged, or maligned at the root level, then we have a much greater chance of truly helping to heal what's wrong. When the core level is healed, symptoms will usually dissipate too.

The larger question for all of us to ask in the battle for our minds is this: *Why?* If we're struggling in our thought lives, what is the root cause of our struggle?

Diagnosing the Spiritual Influenza

The larger question can be phrased different ways.

For instance, you might ask yourself: *What painful thing am I avoiding?* Perhaps a constant irritant or disappointment exists in your life. You seemingly can't avoid it, so you mentally retreat to your fantasy life to escape.

Or you might ask: *What am I so angry about?* The driver who cut you off on the freeway is only a trigger to a deeper anger that isn't resolved. Perhaps someone did a lot of damage to you years

---

[1] Jon Snyder, "Fantasies: The Window to Your Wound," Covenant Eyes, July 31, 2019, https://www.covenanteyes.com/2018/05/31/fantasies-window-to-your-wound.

ago. Ask: What happened? What was taken from you? What in your past is so painful?

Or you might ask: *Why am I on high alert all the time?* What happened that caused you to be in constant protective mode? Who hurt you so much that you're determined never to experience that hurt again?

Or you might ask: *Why do I feel so ashamed?* Did someone hurt you, but you carry the shame as your own? Did you do something but you've never fully accepted Christ's forgiveness? Are you involved in something now that you know isn't right?

A married couple came to my office and asked for help. Garrett was the principal at a Christian school and Amanda worked as an architect at a firm downtown. They were both active in their church, community, and children's lives.

After they sat down, Amanda glanced at her husband, then swung her gaze straight at me and said in a low voice, "Garrett's suddenly developed a problem with porn. I didn't know what to do. I feel hurt and betrayed. I want him to leave. Instead, we came to you."

I looked at Garrett and said, "Tell me about your problem with pornography."

"I feel really ashamed of myself," he said. "I never wanted to hurt my wife. I thought this was under control. Then there's my work. I'm supposed to be setting an example in all areas of my life. I haven't told the superintendent or any of my colleagues—and I haven't looked at porn while on the job, only at home. I didn't want to tell my wife about it, but I knew she would probably find out. It's weird, but I kind of wanted her to know. Everything just seems so out of control right now."

I looked at them both and said, "Amanda used the word 'suddenly' in her initial statement. Can either of you tell me more about what's 'sudden' with this problem?"

Garrett shrugged. "Well, I haven't really struggled with porn until lately. Amanda's been a real trooper in this last season of life. I just got a new job at the start of this year. I transitioned from being vice principal to principal, which is a role I've always wanted to fill. But my days are longer, plus there's a steep learning curve. I wish I could do better at my new job. Also, we just moved across the city to be closer to the school so our kids could attend there in a couple of years. The move meant a lot of stress for everybody. We've got a four-year-old and an eight-month-old baby. Amanda has a demanding job, and she just went back to work after finishing maternity leave. Our new house needed some renovations, so Amanda's been putting in extra hours there, getting permits from the city and whatnot. There's been a lot of upheaval in our family lately. Most days we're just struggling to keep it together."

Let's pause the illustration there, because you can see how we're starting to uncover some of the underlying reasons that Garrett might be looking at porn. The family is dealing with a lot of external pressures at work and home. Life seems out of balance for them as a couple, and for Garrett personally. In his stress, he's crying out for help, seeking consolation. He feels overwhelmed, and he's using porn as a relief mechanism. Amanda sounds like she's under a lot of pressure too, but for now, her stress isn't exhibiting itself symptomatically—at least, not yet.

There are several things they can do immediately to lower the overall stress in their family. Yet ultimately, we'll want to deal with whatever is pulling Garrett toward sin. The root problem is probably more complex than what we've dug up so far. We might find dysfunctional systems in their families of origin. Garrett might have experienced some deep trauma in his past that he hasn't yet revealed. There could be a whole host of issues that we haven't tapped into yet. But right at the start, it feels like we're making some headway in uncovering the root cause.

Hang on, because we need to address two side issues before we can go further.

Important Sidelights

First, some Christian leaders will insist that the process of checking under the hood is a worthless quest. "It's not that complicated," they'll say. "Sin is sin, so let's deal with the sin. Garrett is looking at porn. His problem started with a moral failure. He chose to click on destructive sites. He needs to repent and stop looking at porn. Period."

I'll agree with part of that approach, but only part. Sin is sin, and I concur that the sin aspect of the problem needs to be dealt with. We don't want to reclassify Garrett's moral failure merely as a "mistake" or a "slip-up" or a "sickness." We don't want to excuse the sin in our efforts to dig deeper and address the root cause. Both the sin and the reason for the sin need to be addressed. Both the symptom and the root cause are important. Garrett does need to repent.

But I'll clarify that Garrett's problem did not start with a moral failure. The sin indeed stemmed from an underlying reason. Garrett sought relief because his life felt out of balance, or perhaps there's another reason we haven't uncovered yet. So we must dig and ask *why*. Why did sin seem more pleasant or less painful than the path of righteousness? What was the reason this lie was believed and acted upon?

If we don't ask why, then the problem will never be dealt with in its entirety. The weed might be pulled, but the root will still be there and will cause the weed to return. If we only deal with the symptom but not the root cause, then the next time Garrett becomes overwhelmed, he will likely revert to his same sinful patterns of coping.

The second side issue is this: Christians can be quick to offer advice in a situation like this, but the specific advice that's often offered has been shown over time to be ineffective, biblically inaccurate, and detrimental. It comes in the form of a criticism that's usually directed toward the wife. Misguided people will look at Garrett and Amanda's problem and say: "If only Amanda had paid more attention to Garrett, this problem would be solved. It's Amanda's fault. The burden is on her to have more sex with her husband. Then he wouldn't be looking at porn."

Wrong. The person who succumbs to pornography is responsible for his or her own choices. It is not Amanda's fault. Any person who sins has a responsibility to confess his own sin and be forgiven. Likewise, the sinning spouse has a responsibility to uncover the larger reasons for the sin and prayerfully deal with the root cause.

This faulty advice comes from a misinterpretation of 1 Corinthians 7:2–5, which states:

> But since sexual immorality is occurring, each man should have sexual relations with his own wife, and each woman with her own husband. The husband should fulfill his marital duty to his wife, and likewise the wife to her husband. The wife does not have authority over her own body but yields it to her husband. In the same way, the husband does not have authority over his own body but yields it to his wife.
>
> Do not deprive each other except perhaps by mutual consent and for a time, so that you may devote yourselves

to prayer. Then come together again so that Satan will not tempt you because of your lack of self-control.

This passage shows marriage as an antidote to immorality, and Paul teaches here that spouses have a "duty" to each other sexually. The Greek word for duty is *opheilē*.[2] It means that married people have a "responsibility" to their spouse.

But having a "responsibility" is not the same as being goaded into having sex with your spouse. Sexual coercion—physically, verbally, or by implication—is never God-honoring. The instruction to fulfill one's marital "duty" of 1 Corinthians 7:3 is not meant to be used as a threat, an insistence, or a guilt trip. If sexual activity is demanded, then that is not God-honoring.

Actually, 1 Corinthians 7:3 is for married couples to highly value the physical expressions of love for one another. Paul wrote this passage to believers who were wondering if they should be married in the first place. He's saying that married sex is right and good, and that married couples should stay married if they're already married. He is not issuing a rigorous decree that a spouse can never say no to having sex. There are legitimate reasons for saying no. Spouses come down with colds. Spouses become exhausted or feel overwhelmed with pressures at home or work. Pregnancy and giving birth complicate any number of things. Headaches can happen in any time and place and culture.

Rather, Paul is telling married couples that they were meant for each other sexually. In a loving relationship, each person has agreed not to be selfish. Each person has vowed to care for and love the other. The NKJV translates this verse, "Let the husband *render to*

---

[2] *Strong's Greek Lexicon*, (G3782) "opheilē," Blue Letter Bible, https://www.bluelet-terbible.org/lexicon/g3782/kjv/tr/0-1/.

his wife the affection due her, and likewise also the wife to her husband" (italics added).

I like that translation. The urging is to show affection. Plus, the instruction goes both ways. Husbands—love your wives! Wives—love your husbands! When you are affectionate with a person, you treat them tenderly and kindly. Your affection may involve sexual expression, or not. Sometimes the most loving thing one spouse can say to the other is, "Let's not have sex tonight. I can see you're exhausted."

If Garrett believes he is not receiving enough affection from Amanda, then he can kindly and carefully communicate his desires to her. But he must not blame her for a lack of sex, and he must not use a lack of sex as an excuse to turn toward pornography. Amanda has a responsibility to love her husband, and there may be things she can do to order her world better to make more room for sexual intimacy with him. Still—and I repeat this emphatically—Amanda is not to blame for Garrett's porn use.

The ironic truth of the matter is this: a person's struggles with pornography are seldom about sex in the first place. They're a symptom of a struggle with God.

And that leads us back to the process of checking under the hood.

Beneath the Surface

A middle-aged parent came to me, highly upset. He was furious at his church and fuming at the young minister who led the youth of their church. It took me a while to calm him down enough so he could talk. Finally, he spilled the larger story.

"I went to our youth pastor and told him he needed to start a college group at our church immediately," the man said. "The youth pastor said he didn't have enough resources. I know we're a small church, but I didn't think his answer was good enough. Why did we hire him, anyway? It's his job to take care of our kids! Already he leads the high school group and the junior highers and our children's ministry and the worship team. I understand that he's busy. But surely he could get some volunteers together and start a college group. He's been recommending for years that any college-age students in our church who want to participate in a college group can join the group of a larger church in town. But that needs to change."

"How many college students do you have at your church right now?" I asked.

"Just one," the man muttered. "My daughter."

I paused, then gently asked, "Was your daughter encouraged by your youth pastor to attend the college group of another church?

"Yes," he said.

"And does she go?"

"No."

"Why not?"

"Because she doesn't want to," he said. "She doesn't want anything to do with God right now. She hasn't for years."

"Oh," I said. "You've talked to your daughter about this?"

"Sure."

"And you and your wife have prayed about this, asking God to soften and change your daughter's heart?"

"Absolutely."

"But God is answering your prayer 'no'—at least for now?"

"Yeah."

"Why might God be saying 'no' to this prayer request?"

"I have no idea," the man said. "God's supposed to help us in these situations, isn't He? He has all the power in the universe."

"He does," I said. "Yet He also allows people to make their own decisions about whether or not they follow Him. Do you believe God is allowing your daughter to make her own choices?"

"I suppose."

"Maybe that feels frustrating to you, because you love your daughter and want the best for her, but she's not choosing the best pathway right now."

"I guess."

"Could it be," I suggested, "that you're not so much angry at your youth pastor as you are angry at God?"

He looked at the floor. Tears welled up in his eyes. "That's it exactly," he said. "My wife and I have been praying for so long for our daughter. But God's not doing anything! Why isn't God answering our prayers with a yes?"

Why God, Why?

That's looking under the surface. The bulk of our frustrations directly relates to how we deal with our disappointment with God. I'll say it again, although slightly rephrased: We sin because we are trying to avoid pain, cope with pain, or soothe ourselves after experiencing pain. We are ultimately disappointed with God because we believe He could have prevented the pain in the first place. Rather than continue to trust Him, we take matters into our own hands. We replace our faith with force (becoming angry). Or we replace our faith with escape (retreating to fantasy).

The middle-aged man was filled with anger and sorrow. His thoughts were dominated by rage and grief. He was directing that anger and lament toward his youth minister. Those were all symptoms—and the man was responsible for the choices he made related to his symptoms. Clearly, he needed to apologize to his youth pastor.

Yet when we peered under the hood, we could see something bigger—his deep concern for his daughter, his fear for his daughter's well-being, his anguish over the choices she was making, his struggle with God in prayer, and ultimately his disappointment with God for not answering his prayers the way he wanted.

Most problems in our thought life follow a similar pattern. Disappointment or hurt happens to us. We wonder why God doesn't protect us or our family. Why has God allowed this harmful thing to come into our life? When we examine our symptoms, and then start tracing the reasons for our symptoms, it almost always boils down to some form of the same question at the root: *Why, God, why?*

Why isn't my daughter walking with You, God?
Why am I not more proficient at my new job, God?
God, why did You allow me to experience an assault?
God, why did You allow my parents to get divorced?
God, why did You allow other kids to bully me?
Why did I get so sick, God?
Why did my brother die so young, God?
Why don't people love me like I want to be loved, God?
Why did You allow my business to fail, God?
Why, God, if You love me so much, did You allow me to encounter violence?
Why is my father absent, God?
How could You allow my mother to be so abusive, God?
God, why have I been a victim of so much injustice and brokenness in the world?

All these questions are born out of pain. Fortunately, we can move beyond our "why" questions then prayerfully ask God to heal us and show us new perspectives or pathways we can take. Yet hang on a moment—because before we heal and move forward, we must ask and answer one huge question that's both simple and complex at the same time:

Is God actually good?

No Ordinary Lovingkindness

A child can be taught to sing of God's goodness. But put fifty years on that same child, take that same person through the darkest night of the soul, and will the same person still proclaim that God is good? That's the fuller complexity of this question.

In an earlier chapter, we touched on the book of Ruth. The mother-in-law in the story, Naomi, experiences one hardship after another: Famine in her hometown. A flight to a foreign country. A husband lost. Two sons deceased. Naomi's life turns bitter. At least that's what she tells all the women of Bethlehem when she returns. Everything Naomi touched has gone bad. Is God good even then?

Life turns better for Naomi toward the end of the book. Yet an answer that's deeper than circumstance is shown in the book of Ruth, emerging in the very name and description of God. Three times in Ruth, God is described by the complex Hebrew word *hesed*.[3] It's difficult to fully translate the word into English, but it basically means "steadfast lovingkindness and faithfulness."[4] It's

---

[3] Thanks to Pastor Christian Lindbeck of Hillcrest Church in Bellingham, Washington, for unpacking this idea of *hesed*. See his message: Hillcrest Church, "God's Loving-Kindness Expressed in a Moabite Woman by Christian Lindbeck," YouTube, November 29, 2021, https://www.youtube.com/watch?v=luS9ogr_To8.

[4] *Strong's Hebrew Lexicon*, (H2617) "hesed," Blue Letter Bible, https://www.blueletterbible.org/lexicon/h2617/kjv/wlc/0-1/.

God's unbreakable goodness, a love that never dissipates, even in hard times.

Is God good? This same description of God—*hesed*—is shown way back in Exodus 34:6 when He first reveals His personal name to Moses. "The LORD, the LORD, the compassionate and gracious God, slow to anger, abounding in love and faithfulness." *Hesed* is translated by those two last English words: "love and faithfulness." The CEV renders it this way: "I show great love, and I can be trusted." But even this falls short of the passion and fuller translation of this Hebrew word. It's not merely God's love. It's God's emphatic love. It's God's abounding love. It's God's never ending, never quitting, always present, fully plentiful, fully flourishing, ample, overflowing, and double-portioned love. That's *hesed*. Is God good? The question is answered in God's very name.

Is God good? That's also the main question of the book of Job. Is God still good even when life is not? In a monumental cosmic debate between God and Satan, the integrity of an ancient patriarch named Job is questioned. Job is prosperous, well-respected, and righteous, but Satan claims that the only reason Job loves God so much is because God has blessed him so much—God is paying Job to be good.

God says otherwise. Satan asks for God's permission to remove Job's blessings to see what transpires. God allows the blessings to be removed. One by one, a series of devastating calamities occurs. Job loses his wealth, children, reputation, and health. His wife is furious and distraught. She tells Job to curse God and die. But Job doesn't. He holds fast to his faith that God is good.

Much of the rest of the book shows a series of lengthy earthly conversations in which people try to understand why all the bad happened. Job's friends come around and contend that Job's own sin caused the trouble. But Job insists he's blameless; surely there's another reason for the evil.

Then, toward the end of the book, God speaks—and His answer can feel mysterious. Perhaps it's not as clear or as satisfying an answer as we would like. Essentially, the answer God gives is that God is God, and Job is not God. Period. In other words, God has a greater agenda than can be fully understood—at least some of the time. It's not a snarky answer. The righteousness, omnipotence, and goodness of God involves theology above our paygrade. Sometimes, God chooses to further His plans through suffering. The book concludes with the test being finished. Job's wealth, reputation, and health are restored to him, and he and his wife have more children. In fact, he becomes twice as prosperous as before.

I find it fascinating that in the middle of all the heartache, even though Job never curses God, Job certainly has to work through his own feelings of sorrow, loss, frustration, and anger toward God. In Job 30:20, he laments, "I cry out to you, God, but you do not answer; I stand up, but you merely look at me." Job is honest in his grief. What's significant is that even in his disappointment, he doesn't turn toward sin as a comforter. He still seeks God. God can handle all of the complex, swirling emotions we bring to Him.

Here's a fact: Jesus never promises us problem-free lives. Scripture points to the valley of the shadow of death and the presence of enemies (Psalm 23:4–5), to the earth giving way and the mountains falling into the heart of the sea (Psalm 46:2), and to daily taking up a cross and following Christ (Luke 9:23). In the middle of any of that trouble, we can be tempted in our thoughts to turn away from God.

But God is still good. The protection that God promises to us means that He walks through the valley of the shadow of death with us; He seats us at an abundant table in the presence of our enemies (Psalm 23:4–5). It means that God is a refuge and strength, an ever-present help in trouble, whose voice whispers even in the midst of the calamity, "Be still, and know that I am God" (Psalm 46:1, 10). It means when we lose our life for His sake, we will actually find life (Matthew 10:39b).

Sometimes the only action we know to take—at least initially—is to lament the disappointment in our life. We agree with God that life is not the way it should be. We cry out to God, stymied by God's apparent silence in our difficulty. Our action of lamenting is powerful. We are not falsely trying to put on a cheerful face. We are not trying to sweep aside the difficulty or pretend it isn't there. We are legitimately grieving, sorrowing, or burning with the intensity of troubled emotions.

Jesus lamented. In Matthew 23:37, He mourned over Jerusalem for rejecting the prophets and messengers of God. In Mark 7:18, Jesus wondered aloud in frustration why His disciples were so slow to understand spiritual matters. In John 11:35, Jesus openly wept, sorrowing over the death of Lazarus and joining with the grief of the dead man's two sisters, Mary and Martha.

In each of those circumstances, God had the power to change things for the better—but He didn't. God could have forced Jerusalem to be a spiritually fertile city. He could have sharpened the disciples' spiritual intellect and understanding. He could have kept Lazarus from dying in the first place.

Yet in each of those situations, God's intricate theology was operating. Sometimes, He chooses to further His plans through suffering. Until we marry that difficult truth to the truth of *hesed*—that God is good, and not merely good but emphatically good—we will always be disappointed with God.

Uncover, Lament, Pray

I don't believe in quick, three-step solutions to the complexities of life's problems. But a shorthand phrase can sometimes help us remember a longer and more involved process involved in peering under the surface. If you're looking for a shorthand expression to remember the biblical truths and actions we are looking at in this chapter, it's essentially this: 1) Uncover, 2) Lament, and 3) Pray to go forward.

1. Uncover.

We examine the symptom (perhaps a desire to turn to porn), then trace that action or desire back to its root cause: something caused us pain. Because of our pain, we are longing to be soothed.

We might also want to exhume any false beliefs about God that are leading us toward sin. (Like: *God is not good.*)

We dig up the lies and expose them by seeking the truth from Scripture. We might also want to write down any lies, confess our faulty beliefs to a trusted friend, and write the scriptural truths above the lies.

When we uncover something, we are asking the question: "What's truly causing this problem at the core?"

2. Lament.

When we lament, we simply call the pain what it is—pain. We acknowledge the hurt. We recognize any disappointment with God we might feel for not preventing the pain.

When we lament, we don't try to feel better at first. We don't push the hurt aside or pretend nothing hurtful has happened to us. We simply acknowledge the hurt of a broken world. We are truthful with ourselves and before God. We say, "Ouch, God, this hurts. I wish things were different."

We might stay with the stage of lamenting for a while. Grief can be complex, and it may help to unpack this stage of healing with a trusted counselor. We'll undoubtedly move to more specific solutions or perspectives eventually, but for a while, it's good to simply lament.

In our lament, we might pray something like this:

God, I've uncovered this pain. I have no idea why You allowed this to happen to me (or to us as a family). I cry aloud in my pain. It hurts! I wish this sorrow weren't there! This is not the way life should be!

In my lament, I also acknowledge Your goodness, even now, even when I don't understand why. I know You are good because You say You are good. You are full of steadfast lovingkindness and faithfulness.

Jesus, I turn to You. Please, meet me exactly where I am in this hurt. You are the Great Physician, and I want this problem to be solved. I want this hurt to be healed.

Yet even if it is not healed or healed completely, Your grace is sufficient, and Your power is made perfect in weakness (2 Corinthians 12:9). I will not turn to sin. I will turn only to You. Amen.

3. Pray to go forward.

Prayerfully, we remind ourselves of the emphatic goodness of God, even in our disappointment. We acknowledge that sometimes God chooses to further His plans through suffering. We don't turn toward sin to soothe us. Rather, we turn toward Christ.

In praying, we ask one deliberate question of the Lord: "God, what would You have me do with this situation right now?" This is a prayer for wisdom and discernment, according to James 1:5.

We believe that God has larger plans and purposes for us beyond pain and lament. Our task is to prayerfully seek God's presence in a next step.

As we go forward, God may show us a new perspective about our lamentable situation. He may ask us to change something about our life. He may shine light on a new pathway we can take. We always move forward in conjunction with Him—never in our own power alone. God is good, and we can trust that He will show us a healing perspective or pathway.

For instance, instead of staying stuck in the question: "Why, God, is my marriage so hard?" we can ask: "What do You want me to do, Lord, in this difficult marriage? How do You want me to love my spouse?" Perhaps God will invite us to encourage our spouse or pray for him or her in new ways. Perhaps God will show us new ways we can make our marriage better. Perhaps God will bring a trusted group of friends around us for support. Perhaps God will allow us to understand our spouse in new and deeper ways.

Or instead of continually asking God, "Why have you allowed me to still be single?" we can ask, "God, how do you want me to make the best of my current situation? Is there something You want me to address to make marriage a greater possibility? How can my life be most meaningful if I never marry?"

Or instead of staying frustrated, asking, "God, why is my job so difficult?" we begin to pray, "Lord, what would You have me do in this situation?" Perhaps God will show us different career options. Perhaps God will bring someone into our life we can talk to about our work difficulties. We can trust that God will show us solid options and solutions.

When we pray to move forward, we have addressed the reality of the current situation. Something is not the way it's supposed to be. We have acknowledged and lamented the pain. Now, we pray that God would show us the best way we can either live with this situation or move beyond it. We trust God for His answer.

Sometimes Jesus will offer us a specific solution. Sometimes He will draw us closer to Him and give us more of Himself. In 2 Corinthians 12:7–9, the Apostle Paul prayed three times for a difficulty to be removed from his life. The problem was not removed, but Paul was able to rejoice because he experienced more of the grace and power of Christ.

Take the Time

Here's my encouragement to you: Set aside some specific and undivided time tonight or this weekend for prayer and reflection. Think back through your life. Uncover the hurts. Lament the hurts. Pray that prayer—or a version of it—over each of your hurts. Acknowledge all your deepest hurts before the Lord. Acknowledge His goodness, even in spite of the pain. Allow God to meet you in your honesty. Then, pray to go forward. Ask, "Lord, what would You have me do in this situation? Is there something You want me to learn or change? How do You want me to know You more through this?"

Our call always is to turn toward Christ, even in the midst of asking, "Why, God, why?" His goodness does not depend on the circumstances of life. That's the message of Ruth and Exodus and Job and the gospels—and all throughout the Bible. The abundantly loving nature of God—*hesed*—never changes.

When we begin to grasp that truth, we start to see our hurts being healed at the core. The root cause begins to be addressed. The flu afflicting our soul is dried up. The tuberculosis is done away with. The leukemia is treated. If we become overwhelmed by life's circumstances, we don't need to turn to sinful thoughts to comfort us, because we trust that God is good even though our circumstances have been hurtful. We turn to God instead of focusing on our hurts or turning to pseudo comforts. We fix our eyes on Christ.

Yes, God is good, even though trauma happened to you as a child. Yes, God is good, even though your marriage today isn't what you hoped it would be. Yes, God is good, even though there are huge unmet desires in your life.

Yes, God is good.

A Transformative Mending

Have you heard about the Japanese art of *kintsugi*?

In late fifteenth-century Japan, a shogun named Ashikaga Yoshimasa broke a valuable bowl and sought to have it fixed. Metal staples were used to put the bowl back together again, Frankenstein-style. The shogun could still use the bowl, but the result looked unappealing. In his frustration, Ashikaga Yoshimasa sought skilled artisans who could repair valuable pottery in different ways. The *kintsugi* method was developed.

Today, when precious pieces of pottery break, those pieces aren't thrown away or stapled back together. Instead, using the *kintsugi* method, they're exquisitely repaired using a lacquer resin mixed with gold. The golden lacquer joins the pieces together and colors the pottery with new lines of healing. People can still see where the pottery broke. Yet the golden lines of repair become part of the art itself. The technique is not only a practical fix; it's a magnificent fix.

Journalist Tiffany Ayuda describes *kintsugi* this way: The method is

[B]uilt on the idea that in embracing flaws and imperfections, you can create an even stronger, more beautiful piece of art. Every break is unique and instead of repairing an item like new, the 400-year-old technique actually highlights the "scars" as a part of the design.[5]

In *kintsugi*, the breaks in pottery are not scorned. Rather, they are honored as part of the pottery's history. The blemishes are respected. In the end, the pottery becomes even more distinctive, even more precious.

Trauma isn't hidden. Trauma is transformed.

Similarly, the heartache that has happened to us does not need to lead us to despair. When we are broken, we are not thrown away. The disappointments we experience do not need to generate within us a destructive thought life.

Instead, when we turn to Jesus, He binds up our wounds (Hosea 6:1). He renews our strength (Isaiah 40:31). He restores what the locusts have eaten (Joel 2:25). He gives a hope and a future (Jeremiah 29:11). He gives us rest when we are weary (Matthew 11:28). He fills us with joy and peace as we trust in Him, so that we may overflow with hope by the power of the Holy Spirit (Romans 15:13). He restores us and makes us strong, firm, and steadfast (1 Peter 5:10). He empowers us to give us victory and overcome the world (1 John 5:4).

Jesus repairs our broken pieces with gold.

---

[5] Tiffany Ayuda, "How the Japanese Art of Kintsugi Can Help You Deal with Stressful Situations," NBC News, April 28, 2018, https://www.nbcnews.com/better/health/how-japanese-art-technique-kintsugi-can-help-you-be-more-ncna866471.

Key Takeaways

- Just as a person can display a symptom of a physical malady, he or she can also display a symptom of a spiritual malady. Most sin is symptomatic of a deeper hurt in our life. We turn to sin to soothe the deeper hurt. The symptomatic sin must be dealt with, but so must the root cause that's triggering the sin. Otherwise, if we don't deal with the root, the same pattern of sin will just keep reappearing in our life.

- Almost all pain has a thread attached to disappointment with God. We expected God to prevent pain from happening to us, yet He allowed pain. We must grapple with the complex truth that God sometimes allows pain to further His agenda. God is still good, even though He allows harmful things to happen to people.

- Once we uncover the source of our pain, we can lament the disappointment, just as Jesus modeled for us. In lamenting, we turn to God for comfort. Through our prayers, Jesus meets us in our disappointment and sadness. Our root malady begins to heal. The symptoms clear up as the root is healed. We can pray to go forward, believing that Christ will offer us a new perspective or pathway.

CHAPTER 6

Shout for Truth

The worship leader at a recent conference astonished me with his talent and versatility. He sat at an acoustic piano with a microphone and simply began to play and sing. He didn't use any sheet music. No band backed him up. He led a few songs on his own, then paused and asked the audience to call out favorites—and to keep calling them out until he had seven songs.

I speak at conferences a lot, and I've seen a lot of worship leaders in action. Asking for favorites is something we used to do thirty years ago when hymnbooks were the norm, when we had a smaller, more familiar collection of songs to choose from. If a worship leader could read music, there was never a danger of not knowing a song. But we weren't using hymnbooks at this conference, there were a lot of young adults present, and this guy was asking for any favorite of any worship song ever known. I mean, there are literally thousands of worship songs to choose from these days.

Audience members called out the titles of songs. Some I recognized; most I didn't. People had come from all over the region, so it wasn't like the worship leader was asking the congregants at his home church to choose from favorites they sang each week. He wasn't trying to show off, either. He asked for the favorites in a spirit of reverence, worship, and prayer, as the Holy Spirit led.

The worship leader wrote down each title on a piece of paper in front of him, then started up again—skillfully playing and singing each song on the list. Amazingly, he wove them together in one continuous medley. We probably worshipped this way for forty minutes straight. The music never stopped, and it was remarkable how after a song started, enough people knew the words so we could all sing together. Sometimes it felt like he was ending one song, but then he'd launch into the chorus of another we'd already sung. The effect was brilliant. As I glanced around the audience, I could see people drawn mightily into the presence of God.

The worship session concluded, and I took the platform to speak. Afterward, I met the worship leader at the front corner of the auditorium. I thanked him for his leadership and noticed he was older than I'd first thought, maybe in his mid-fifties. I asked him about the technique he'd used of calling for favorites—if he'd actually memorized every worship song ever written.

"Ha! Not hardly," he said with a chuckle.

"But you've memorized so many songs!" I exclaimed. "It's incredible."

"I depend on the Holy Spirit to lead the people to call out the songs that He wants used," he said. "And I'm also confident about the countless hours I've put in practicing. Each morning I practice piano, singing, and worship leading for about two hours. All that practicing adds up over the years. God uses our practice sessions—I have no doubt about it."

"Wow, intriguing," I said. "Tell me more."

"Back when I was a kid, I started taking piano lessons from our pastor's wife," he said. "The first thing she instructed me to do—even before I played one note—was memorize Hebrews 5:14. Do you know it offhand?"

I shook my head

"'Solid food is for the mature, who because of practice have their senses trained to distinguish between good and evil.'" He quoted it from the NASB.

I nodded.

"My teacher stressed that all the practice we do for the sake of Christ is important," he added. "No matter if we're playing the piano or developing our faith, God uses our practice sessions for the sake of His glory."

The Power of Four

Practice means to repeat something over and over. We immerse ourselves in the skill or subject as if we're soaking in a hot tub. In consideration of that immersion, this chapter's encouragement might sound basic at first, the spiritual equivalent of getting our toes wet by the water's edge. But I don't want us to gloss over this, because there's an important twist to it. The encouragement is simply this: Do we want to win the battles in our mind? Then we need to read the Bible.

Here's the twist. I encourage us to read the Bible, and read the Bible, and read the Bible again. We can't simply skim over its pages once or twice. When it comes to putting the truths of Scripture into our minds so we are transformed by Christ, we need to stay at it continually. We need to dive into the deep end.

Here's why. People quote John 8:32 all the time—"The truth will set you free"—but they typically quote it out of context, or only a sliver of it, which doesn't convey its fuller truth.

"Okay sure, you gotta get yourself some truth," people say. "That truth will do wonders in your life."

Yes. But here's the fuller context. The promise of John 8:32 comes with an important condition. It's shown in an "if-then" statement, which is found in the previous verse, John 8:31. Here are both verses together:

> To the Jews who had believed him, Jesus said, "If you hold to my teaching, you are really my disciples. Then you will know the truth, and the truth will set you free."

Do you see the condition? "If you hold to my teaching.... Then you will know the truth, and the truth will set you free." We can't ignore the "if." As the fuller context points out, we must hold to Jesus's teaching for the truth to impact us. We must grasp that truth tightly. We must take it in like food we eat every day. We must ingest that truth as if at a molecular level.

We absorb Scripture by constant and mindful repetition. We read the Bible over and over again, continually filling our minds with God's truth, reminding ourselves of what He wants us to know. We hold to Jesus's teaching by committing ourselves to the habit of regular Bible reading. We read the Scriptures daily the same way the worship leader practiced every morning. God uses our practice sessions for His glory.

It might sound strange to hear, but the benefits of repeated exposure to the Bible have actually been proven statistically. Dr. Pamela Caudill Ovwigho and Dr. Arnold Cole from the Center for Bible Engagement conducted detailed research. Using a diverse mix of open-ended questions, they surveyed more than four hundred thousand Americans to determine religious beliefs, religious service attendance, daily temptations, risky and moral behavior, and beliefs about spiritual growth and maturity. They crunched the numbers and revealed three important findings.

First, "Scripture engagement more reliably predicts moral behavior than traditional measures of spirituality, such as church attendance and prayer."[1] In other words, Bible reading definitely affects how we live.

Second, that believers who "read or listen to the Bible at least four days a week" think and act measurably differently than those who engage with the Bible less often.[2] The number four is significant. Not three, not two, not one. But four.

Third, when Christians passed the important "number three" threshold and went into their fourth engagement with the Bible each week, they reported a significantly positive difference in how they coped with hard times. Specifically:

- Use of pornography and involvement in other sexual sins dropped 62 percent.
- Relational issues (especially in marriage) dropped 40 percent.
- Feelings of loneliness dropped 30 percent.
- Anger issues dropped 32 percent.
- Alcoholism dropped 57 percent.
- Feelings of spiritual stagnation dropped 60 percent.[3]

---

[1] Pamela Caudill Ovwigho and Arnold Cole, "Understanding the Bible Engagement Challenge: Scientific Evidence for the Power of 4," Center for Bible Engagement, December 2009, https://bttbfiles.com/web/docs/cbe/Scientific_Evidence_for_the_Power_of_4.pdf.

[2] Ibid.

[3] See also https://www.centerforbibleengagement.org/research.

The statistics show it. If we open our Bible only once a week at church, then the impact on our life won't be large. Nor can we merely flip open our Bibles two or three times a week and expect things to change.

When we read our Bibles four days per week, significant transformation begins to occur. If we read the Bible more days per week, that's even better. We must get into God's Word so God's Word gets into us.

Of course, God is a Person and not bound by a statistic—and the Word of God is living and active, not bound to a statistic, either. Yet numbers can reflect upward or downward trends, and the numbers show that when believers read their Bibles a minimum of four times a week, that's when transformation begins to happen. That's typically when the "if-then" condition of John 8:31–32 kicks in and we begin to *hold fast* to Jesus's teaching. We become the product of our habits. The truth gets into us, and the truth sets us free.

Pathways of God's Commands

A colleague asked about the writing project I was working on, and I described to him the premise of this book.

"Hmm," he said. "Sounds like a book about sin management."

I had to think for a moment, then responded, "No, that's not the final takeaway for readers. The emphasis isn't on 'sin management,' just like I wouldn't want to write a book on 'anger management.' Why manage something when it can be eliminated? We're dealing with the source of a problem, not just a symptom. The takeaway is that readers can live fully and abundantly, as Jesus invited us to, continually filling our minds and hearts with the thoughts of God. It's an invitation to true freedom and a new quality of life."

Psalm 119:32 came to mind, one of my favorite verses, and I quoted it to him from the older (1984) version of the NIV, which is how I learned it: "I run in the path of your commands, for you have set my heart free." We had a good discussion about the paradoxical wording of that verse.

"Commands" and "free" are two words that often stand in opposition to one another, but in this case, they help express a significant truth. If someone commands us to do something and we must do it, how does that result in freedom?

Soldiers are regularly commanded by their superior officers. If a sergeant orders a private to dig a foxhole, then that foxhole better get dug. If a lieutenant orders a platoon of soldiers to advance toward the enemy and open fire, then they'd better advance, guns blazing. Soldiers certainly can't do whatever they want, whenever they want. Although they might live in or fight for a free country, in many senses of the word, soldiers are not "free."

History has shown that the Communist officials of the former USSR tried their hardest to command people to live in certain ways. Citizens of that country didn't have the rights of free speech or expression. They couldn't worship the way they wanted. The freedom of the press was severely curtailed. The government controlled people's housing, education, and occupations. If you didn't like how things were run, then tough—you were sent to Siberia. The Russian people longed to shake off their "commands" and be "free."

We often define freedom as the ability to do whatever we want to do, whenever we want to do it. But that's not true freedom, that's anarchy—and it's not how the word is used in Psalm 119:32. The freedom defined by that verse and others in the Bible is the freedom to "truly live" (1 Thessalonians 3:8). When we keep in step with God, the restraints and confines of sin don't hamper us. When we "walk by the Spirit," we will not "gratify the desires of the flesh" (Galatians 5:16), and that frees us from the hindrances that result from sin.

The commands of God benefit us. It's in our best interest to keep them—even enthusiastically. Like the psalmist, we're not merely *walking* in the paths of God's commands, we're *running*. When God gives us a command, it's never to squash us under His thumb. His commands don't lead to suffering and repression, and they don't make us miserable. Rather, the commandments of God allow us to live abundantly.

Consider how the keeping of any number of commands can lead to freedom and happiness. Nobody complains about the command to drive on the correct side of the street. When we all follow the directives of modern law, we can all drive to where we need to go.

If we want to enjoy the incredible freedom of movement that a sport such as snowboarding offers, we must first subject ourselves to the command of restraint. We must strap our boots to the board. Then we must subject ourselves to the discipline of learning how to snowboard.

Caring parents command their children not to drink drain cleaner or play on busy streets. When a command comes from a loving or benevolent authority, it can be a very good thing.

Similarly, if we are living by the command to "take captive every thought and make it obedient to Christ" (2 Corinthians 10:5b) and then replace illicit thoughts with those that align with the imperatives of Philippians 4:8—to think about whatever is true, noble, right, pure, lovely, admirable, excellent, or praiseworthy—then we can run in the freedom of Isaiah 26:3 NLT: "You will keep in perfect peace all who trust in you, all whose thoughts are fixed on you!"

The commands of God help us win the battles of our mind.

Actions of Practice

A clear passage that shows the effects of repeated Scripture immersion and its positive effects on our thought life is Psalm 119:9–16. The context is our spiritual formation. The passage mentions young people specifically, but the Bible's benefits are not limited to any age group. As you read the portion of Scripture below, notice the multitude of actions the psalmist mentions.

> How can a young person stay on the path of purity?
> By living according to your word.
> I seek you with all my heart;
> do not let me stray from your commands.
> I have hidden your word in my heart
> that I might not sin against you.
> Praise be to you, LORD;
> teach me your decrees.
> With my lips I recount
> all the laws that come from your mouth.
> I rejoice in following your statutes
> as one rejoices in great riches.
> I meditate on your precepts
> and consider your ways.
> I delight in your decrees;
> I will not neglect your word.

What actions does the psalmist take? He lives according to God's Word. He's careful not to stray from God's commandments. He hides the Word in his heart. He invites God to teach him His decrees. He speaks about Scripture. He rejoices in following God's statutes. He highly values Scripture. He meditates on God's Word. He delights in Scripture. He pledges not to neglect God's Word. He practices running after the pathways of God's commands, for that is when his heart is freed.

Why is it so important to read the Bible again and again? Consider how the Bible is not simply a moral book, or even merely a wise book. Hebrews 4:12 says,

> For the word of God is alive and active. Sharper than any double-edged sword, it penetrates even to dividing soul and spirit, joints and marrow; it judges the thoughts and attitudes of the heart.

That means the Holy Spirit constantly works in conjunction with the Scripture we put in our minds.

God's Word is the necessary ingredient for spiritual formation. Acts 20:32 describes how "the word of his grace can build you up." And 2 Timothy 3:16–17 says,

> All Scripture is God-breathed and is useful for teaching, rebuking, correcting and training in righteousness, so that the servant of God may be thoroughly equipped for every good work.

We need to regularly immerse ourselves in God's word so we can be built up, taught, rebuked or corrected (if it's for our own good), and trained in righteousness.

The Bible is so important that Jesus classified God's Word as the necessary ingredient for life itself. In Matthew 4:4, Christ referenced Deuteronomy 8:3. "It is written: 'Man shall not live on bread alone, but on every word that comes from the mouth of God.'"

That's how important the Bible is. Do we want to have a better thought life? Then we must continually fill our mind with God's thoughts. It's that simple.

For twenty-three years, Dr. Woodrow Kroll served as president and senior Bible teacher at the international radio ministry Back to the Bible. He was intrigued by an excuse that he frequently heard when people were asked if they had ever read the Bible. They often responded: "I don't have enough time." So Dr. Kroll wanted to see if that was actually valid. He conducted an experiment and wrote about it afterward:

> I set out to find out how much time it actually takes to read the entire Bible cover to cover. Over the course of several months, every free hour I had, every plane trip I took, every moment of down time, I read my Bible and timed myself as I read it. I literally hung a stopwatch around my neck like a football coach and set out to time how long it took to read every book in the Bible.
>
> Without speed reading, at a leisurely pace, and clicking my stopwatch to pause every time I was interrupted and then clicking it again as I returned to read, I discovered that a person can read the entire Bible in fewer than 72 hours.
>
> In fact, half the books of the Bible can be read in less than 30 minutes each; 26 of them can be read in less than 15 minutes each.

It seems astounding to me that a person can live 85 years and still say "I don't have time" to read all the way through the only book God ever wrote.

My conclusion was that it is not a valid excuse.[4]

Nostalgia, Mindreading, and Extremes

So we need to read the Bible, and read it some more, and then read it again. We need to apply ourselves diligently to Scripture so the truth gets into our thoughts. If we do that, then the truth lodges its way in our mind and can set us free.

Let's look at three specific applications of how God's Word can set us free.

1. Scripture helps us overcome the lies of nostalgia.

Social media sites allow us to keep up with people from our past—including people we dated or once had strong feelings for. We can know continuing facts and anecdotes about them that we would not have been able to know in generations past. But if we are married and pursuing other people online in any way, we are betraying our spouse. If we are single and pursuing a former love who's now married, the Bible refers to that as lurking at our neighbor's door (Job 31:9). It's harmful and must be stopped. We must delete any site that tempts us toward infidelity.

It's not wrong to be nostalgic or to feel sentimental about the past. But nostalgia can betray us, because it's too easy to look upon the past and remember only the idealized versions of things, the

---

[4] Dr. Woodrow Kroll, *The New Christian Spirituality*, unpublished manuscript, 177.

things we selectively choose to remember. We see a picture of a former significant other online; that person is looking good, and we catch ourselves in a moment of longing.

"Wow," we say. "We never should have broken up. We sure had some good times back then, didn't we?"

Or did you?

You undoubtedly did have some good times with your former significant other. But you had some crummy times, too. Ultimately, something in the relationship didn't work, which led to the breakup. Either you weren't committed to the other person, or the other person wasn't committed to you. That was serious. That was real. Remember: You broke up for a reason.

If all we do is obsess over a past relationship, then we are not growing or being present and available for a healthy relationship today. Our mind becomes littered with broken memories and false hopes. Past relationships can be tricky, because there's a sense where a person we once cared for will always have a place in our heart. Yet it's also true that we must untether our heart from our past. We find balance when we instruct ourselves to always view a past relationship through the lens of truth. The relationship didn't work out, and it didn't work out for a reason. We are certainly not called to *hate* our ex. No. It's okay to think of an ex warmly, under the umbrella of honest, Christ-honoring friendship and care. That person was deeply important to us in a certain season of life. But that season is over now, and we need to move on. A mind can't be permitted to wander without limits.

When it comes to our important relationships today, we must always be on guard, erring on the side of caution. Researchers from Boston University and the Pontificia Universidad Católica de Chile showed that frequent use of social media sites is "negatively correlated with marriage quality and happiness, and positively correlated with experiencing a troubled relationship and thinking about divorce."[5]

Ecclesiastes 7:10 NLT lays it out plainly: "Don't long for 'the good old days.' This is not wise." If we're always thinking about the past, then we're focusing on things we can never attain. If we're constantly longing for the past, then we're not focused on the present. We're not fully loving the one we're with.

Perusing social media sites isn't wrong in itself. But we must be careful about those sites and our thought life. That means willfully deciding not to ogle any former significant other online. We deliberately refuse to let our mind go there. We must be honest with ourselves and make the tough choices for the greater good. Although social media is not harmful for everybody, we all must ask: "Is social media harmful for me?" Then make the choice.

2. Scripture puts an end to mindreading.

Used in the psychological sense, "mindreading" is also "second guessing" or "jumping to conclusions." This can happen if we hear a snippet of conversation, or if we make a few observations about a person or a situation and then become fully convinced we know what someone else is thinking, what happened, or why they acted the way they did.

We can be so quick to create narratives in our heads. We experience a situation, interpret it in our mind, and create a story around it that fits what we want to believe. That narrative becomes

---

[5] Sebastián Valenzuela, Daniel Halpern, and James Katz, "Social Network Sites, Marriage Well-Being and Divorce: Survey and State-Level Evidence from the United States," *Computers in Human Behavior* 36 (July 2014): 94–101, https://doi.org/10.1016/j.chb.2014.03.034.

the framework by which we live and act. But what if our interpretation is off? Perhaps the story we created isn't fact at all.

Maybe we sent a text to our friend Jo-Jo, but Jo-Jo didn't text us back quickly enough. We jump to the conclusion that Jo-Jo doesn't like us. Or that Jo-Jo is angry at us. What's the truth?

Maybe Jo-Jo was in the hospital and couldn't get to his phone.

Maybe Jo-Jo was out of town and in a business meeting all day.

Maybe Jo-Jo dropped his phone in the toilet and hasn't been able to power it up ever since. Hey, it happens.

Or perhaps we say hello to our friend Brunhilda at church, but she gets an odd look on her face and exclaims: "Oh, this isn't good!"—something we didn't expect to hear. Later we rehash the conversation mentally. We conclude that Brunhilda is weird, and we vow to keep our distance from her.

But maybe Brunhilda got that peculiar look due to a bad slice of pizza she ate for breakfast that just came back to bite her. She used that negative phrase because she was just about to run to the bathroom to hurl.

Or maybe Brunhilda was troubled because she was thinking about a troubling trend in the culture—something completely unrelated to our hello.

Perhaps we're browsing online and see a video of our colleague, Rico. He's got a huge piece of chocolate cake in his hand and he's dancing on top of his desk at work. We conclude that we weren't invited to a terrific party. Or we falsely predict that Rico is a real lush and bound to get fired soon.

But maybe it was an elaborate prank for the boss. Or maybe Rico was acting out what he saw in a movie. Maybe he just gets really excited about eating cake. And maybe we're just plain wrong.

When we regularly study Scripture, we can remind ourselves that we "should be quick to listen, slow to speak, and slow to become angry" (James 1:19). The truth sets us free.

With that verse in mind, we can allow ourselves the time to correctly make decisions and to suspend judgment if we don't have all the facts. According to James 1:5, we can pray and ask the Lord for wisdom in any situation. So we know it's prudent to ask people for clarification. With God's Word in mind, we are more apt to reframe our thoughts about a person or a situation according to truth.

3. Scripture helps us balance our thinking.

Have you ever noticed how people are prone to lean toward extremes? It's easy to lean one way and assume worst-case scenarios, or to lean the other direction and become apathetic. One helpful diagram I've used over the years shows how to balance our thinking.[6]

I draw a line on a piece of paper, and on one far side I write this word: *catastrophe.*

—————————CATASTROPHE

When our minds are programmed to think "catastrophe," we lean toward viewing all our problems in an overly important or impactful light. We make things out to be worse than they actually are. Like, "Oh no, my friend said such and such, and now it's the end of the relationship!" Few things in life are actually catastrophes. We need to avoid this extreme.

---

[6] The diagram came from Dr. Earl Wilson, Ph.D., during his time at Western Seminary.

On the other side of the paper, to signify the opposite end of the spectrum, I write another word: *indifference.*

INDIFFERENCE————————CATASTROPHE

Another harmful extreme that we can lean toward in our thinking is the tendency to shrug things off. Genuine problems do occur, but in the indifference mode we pretend the problems are no big deal. Like, "Hey, I've got terminal cancer. Oh well. Easy come, easy go."

That doesn't work either. When problems occur, they are valid, and if something is harming us or even just annoying us, it should be dealt with. We need to avoid the extremes in our thought life of indifference. In the middle of the sheet, I write a final word: *reality.*

INDIFFERENCE————REALITY————CATASTROPHE

Reality is the balance to aim for. Problems are seldom catastrophic, but at the same time, we don't want to be indifferent to them, either. The balance is to seek reality, see problems in perspective, learn what we can do about life's hard stuff, and discern what we simply need to let lie.

That diagram has helped me tremendously. When the stuff of life happens, it's wise to sort out an appropriate response.

When a genuine problem arises, we don't shrug it off and say, "That's no big deal." Similarly, we avoid the other extreme, and don't cry out, "Oh no! It's the end of the world!"

We figure out what reality actually looks like, and work from there. We figure out reality either from speaking to trusted advisors or from our own logic and discernment. Proverbs 11:14 says, "For lack of guidance a nation falls, but victory is won through many advisors." And Ephesians 4:15 encourages us to speak the truth in love. We need to speak the truth in love to others—and to ourselves.

That leads to a balanced perspective.

Shout for Truth

The task of reading our Bible and filling our minds with God's truth isn't hard. But it does require repetition.

We've looked several times already at the incident when Jesus was tempted in the wilderness. Notice that He took every thought captive and resisted the devil by answering with Scripture. Jesus grabbed the lie, examined the lie and saw it for a lie, then announced to Himself—and to the devil—the truth.

We can do this, too. Let's put the action to take into a memorable phrase. When an illicit thought comes into our mind, we can "shout for truth." We can take every thought captive and resist the devil by answering with the truth of Scripture. We can reframe a faulty narrative to align with truth.

This works for sexual temptation. For example, perhaps we're scrolling through social media and we're tempted to think illicit thoughts about a person we used to date. Or we're surfing online and we're enticed to seek inappropriate images. When this temptation occurs, we shout for truth. We ask ourselves a very simple question: "Does this thought align with God's best for my life?" We take every thought captive and specifically ask God for help to resist the temptation. Then we remind ourselves of a pertinent Bible verse—perhaps, Proverbs 5:16: "May you rejoice in the wife (or husband) of your youth." We reframe the faulty narrative and replace it with the truth.

This works if we have a tendency to overthink things, or assume the worst about a person, or second-guess what we did or said. If we're not careful, it's easy to find ourselves in a spiral. A woman I know was a well-paid attorney with a loving husband and three well-adjusted teenage children, and they lived in a comfortable home. She regularly enjoyed her hobby of long-distance running, and was well loved and respected by her circle of friends and colleagues at church and work.

Yet, she described to me how she often felt like an imposter. Other attorneys were more qualified than her, she insisted. She felt guilty about not spending enough time with her kids, and she worried that she neglected her husband. Her house was too messy. Her running times weren't fast enough. She was positive her friends were saying bad things behind her back.

We began to reframe her life in light of the truth. Through counseling, she began to see that she wasn't an imposter. She had every right to be working at her firm at the high level she was. She saw how she could be thankful for what she had—rather than unhappy about what she didn't have. She began to remind herself daily of her worth in Christ—that she was a beloved child of God—and she soaked her mind in the truth of 1 John 4:16a, "And so we know and rely on the love God has for us." When she unpacked conversations and times when she believed her friends were saying bad things about her, she was able to see that they weren't actually saying those things—it was only her suspicions. The more she examined her thoughts and told herself the truth, the more her life began to change.

This can work for the normal anxieties of life. A good friend travels a lot for work but hates to fly. Early one morning his wife was driving him to the airport, and the man mentioned that he was feeling quite anxious about the trip. A big contract was on the line, and he wanted to make sure everything was right.

"Do you have any encouragement for me this morning from Scripture?" he asked.

His wife quoted Philippians 4:6–7, "Do not be anxious about anything, but in every situation, by prayer and petition, with thanksgiving, present your requests to God. And the peace of God, which transcends all understanding, will guard your hearts and your minds in Christ Jesus."

Right then in the car, zipping along on the freeway to the airport, they prayed about the trip, presenting their requests to God. At the airport and during the flight, the man meditated on the truth continually, replaying that verse in his mind over and over again. After he reached his hotel that night, he was still deliberately soaking in God's truth. Instead of letting his mind run away with his fears about his meetings the next day, he reminded himself that God was in control. Sure, he needed to prepare for his meeting. Yet God was lavishly pouring over him a peace that transcended all understanding.

He slept well that night.

And he got the contract.

Key Takeaways

- To win the battles in our thought life, we need to fill our mind with the Word of God. The truth of God's Word sets us free. But there's an if-then condition attached to the promise where it's found in John 8:31–32. Only when we "hold to" the teachings of Christ can we know the truth and be set free by it. We need to read Scripture, and read Scripture, and read it again.
- God uses our practice sessions for the sake of His glory. Research shows that we need to read the Bible a minimum of four times per week for the most amount of positive change to occur in our life.

- When an illicit thought comes into our mind, we can "shout for truth." We can take every thought captive and resist the devil by answering with the truth of Scripture. We can reframe a faulty narrative so it aligns with truth.

CHAPTER 7

The Structurally Wise Life

O nce upon a time, a man went to see his counselor.

"Hey there," the man said. "I hope you can help. My life is chaotic and troubled. Regularly I get big purple bruises and welts all over my face. I have massive headaches. My teeth crack often. And about once a quarter, I break my nose."

"Hmmm," said the counselor. "What do you think is causing all this pain and trouble in your life?"

"That's simple," said the man. "I keep hitting myself in the head with a hammer."

"Oh," said the counselor. "Maybe you should stop."

"Well," said the man, "here's where it gets difficult. It's a terrific stress reliever. I like the feeling of power and control when I do this. I get some kind of huge chemical rush whenever I hit my face with a hammer—adrenaline or endorphins or something. All I know is I've tried to stop many times, but I can't. The truth is..." The man paused, as if searching for the right words to follow.

The counselor nodded. "Go on."

The man swallowed hoarsely then added, "When it comes to hitting myself with a hammer, I enjoy it."

Surfacing Illogic

That story is a parable, but I hope you see how it paints a picture of any kind of destructive living. We are desperate for a change to occur in our life, but we enjoy our current behavior even though we cognitively know and agree that it's destructive. This pattern of problematic thinking is evident whenever we entertain pornographic thoughts, overeat to the point of hurting our health, mire ourselves in thoughts of revenge, allow jealous thoughts to destroy a relationship, worry to the point of developing an ulcer, or entertain anger at such a level that we explode with rage and damage our career, family, or reputation.

Too many times we hear impassioned pleas for logical thinking—as if logic alone will solve our problems. We hear this plea from pastors, counselors, friends, and family members. We read it in books. We hear it in seminars. The plea for logical thinking basically follows this ultra-simple pattern: A) If we understand that certain behaviors cause great harm, then B) we will stop those behaviors. The logic seems linear and sound. The assumption is that people are rational, and A always leads to B.

But A doesn't always lead to B—not in real life. If logical thinking alone could solve our problems, then why do people still smoke cigarettes? The advice-givers fail to realize that our wish to stay in our problems defies logical thinking. Our grasp of logic doesn't always prompt us to stop harmful behaviors. It's severely illogical to hit yourself in the face with a hammer and refuse to stop, but this kind of behavior happens all the time in different ways and by various means. Have you ever told yourself something like this?

- I know pornography is harmful to me, but I keep viewing it anyway.
- I realize I should eat a balanced diet and regularly exercise, but that's hard to do. I'd rather watch a football game on TV than go outside and play touch football with my son. Besides, I like to eat junk food. I might be on the path toward heart disease and a stroke, but there's no way I'm ever going to give up potato chips and cake.
- I understand that I shouldn't hold grudges, but I love the feeling of mentally replaying a heated argument. In my mind, I dish out stormy comebacks and destroy my opponent with full-on wrath and razor-sharp putdowns.
- I can see how I shouldn't be jealous of my friend, but did you see what she posted online today? She's always been handed everything. She's so spoiled. I can't stand her.
- I try so hard not to worry, but if I can't worry, then what can I do? Worrying gives me a feeling of control. If I worry, at least I'm doing something.
- I know it's in my best interest to stay calm behind the wheel of my car, but that jerk just cut me off. I'm going to speed up, cut him off, lean on my horn, and flip him an obscene gesture. Road rage feels so justified sometimes.

That's illogical thinking at work. That's hitting ourselves in the face with a hammer. Engaging in the harmful behavior feels rational because we want to justify our actions and make a case for behaving poorly. But the big-picture logic is completely wrong. We mentally agree that a specific pattern of thinking or behavior is harmful, yet we choose destruction over benefit anyway. Whenever we choose harm over health, that is illogical.

What we need is a solution that extends beyond the oft-heard pleas for logical thinking. It's a solution that is based in logic but goes beyond. It says, "Hey, it doesn't matter whether or not I *enjoy* this destructive behavior, I am going to stop."

The starting point to overturning illogical thinking is to allow Christ to ask us a simple question that reveals our truest interests, our deepest longings. Answering this question clarifies for us that we truly do want life to be better. Until we answer Christ's question with a sincere *yes*, we will never change. What's the question?

When Jesus Asks an Important Question

As Jesus walked through the dusty streets of Jerusalem on a Sabbath, He entered an area of the city near the Sheep Gate, the place where officials scrutinized animals brought to the temple for sacrifice to ensure they were blemish-free. It was a telling location, because Jesus was the True Spotless Lamb of God who had come to take away the sins of the world.

John 5:1–5 records the rest of the story. Near the Sheep Gate lay a pool called Bethesda. Large crowds of infirm people—the blind and broken, the wounded and withered—lay near the pool, waiting, aching, longing for life to be different, hoping to be first into the water. All desperate for change. The pool was said to have supernatural healing powers. Every so often the water bubbled up, and the first person to jump in the water was healed.

One man with a faraway look in his eyes lay near the pool. He was unable to walk, and he was all alone. Any person without the use of his legs was at a disadvantage. Any person with nobody to help him into the water surely would have a difficult time being first into the pool.

Jesus noticed the man and understood he'd been in this condition for a long time. Thirty-eight hard years. His state seemed so hopeless—at least to most people. A healing was surely on the horizon, but when Jesus walked up to him and spoke, the answer to Jesus's question seemed ridiculously obvious at first.

"Do you want to get well?"

Well, *duh.* Why would Jesus ever ask a question with such a patently plain answer?

Perhaps because the answer wasn't obvious to the man. Perhaps because the man had forgotten his true goal. Perhaps because the man needed to be reminded of what he truly wanted in his deepest being. Perhaps because Jesus doesn't force His healing on anyone; He wanted to have the man's agreement that life for him would change and that change would be a desirable thing.

We can almost see the man's mind at work. *Do I want to get well, or do I want to stay lying on this crummy mat for the rest of my life? Sure, I want to get well, but lying on this mat is all I know. It's no way to live, but at least it's familiar. What might happen if I get up from this mat? Do I really want my life to be changed?*

The man needed to be reminded of his core desire. He needed to be snapped back to truly logical thinking. At his core, the man didn't want to remain in his hopeless state. If he was ever going to be healed, he needed to insist that he was finished lying on the mat. He needed to be firm in his resolve to change.

The same answer is required from us. If we remain in a desperate condition for a long time, it can be easy to forget what we truly long for. It's easy to stay where we are, lying on our metaphoric mat, unmoving in our hopeless state. At least the hopeless state is familiar.

When we focus on Christ, He asks if we want to change. Our willingness is required. As we continue to look to Him and rely on His power, Christ provides hope and renews our strength. With Christ's help, we can see that our situation is not hopeless after all. Jesus shows us that our habit is not unbreakable. We do not need to give in to that familiar sin. If we listen closely, we can hear His voice in our ears, reminding us of what we truly long for at our core:

"Do you want to get well?"

Yes! Thanks to Jesus, we can indeed say yes to that question. First Corinthians 10:13 NLT makes this abundantly clear.

> The temptations in your life are no different from what others experience. And God is faithful. He will not allow the temptation to be more than you can stand. When you are tempted, he will show you a way out so that you can endure.

In other words, the sin that tempts us isn't all-powerful. It isn't original, either, and it isn't unique to us. The mind is a place for battle in every believer's life, but the sin that besieges us doesn't need to win. God is faithful, and no temptation needs to conquer us, because sin contains no imperative for believers, thanks to Christ's work on the cross. Nobody is forcing us to sin. There is always a way out. Even if we enjoy the rush of the hammer, we are not forced to bash our face in.

So we must answer Christ's question with, "Yes! I want to get well!" Harm is harm, and we must not stay in the harm. We need to see that we are finished with lying on a mat in a state of hopelessness. When we are tempted to choose pornography—or any harmful thought—even if that thought creates an adrenaline rush that offers a momentary high, we have to say, "Wait a minute! I do not want this. I am certain of what I truly want. I want to get well!"

A Series of Wise Decisions

So we are learning how to overcome our illogical desires to remain in sin. Throughout this book, we are addressing the frameworks of our life that prompt us to keep choosing the hammer in the face. We are reminding ourselves that the Bible contains the promise that we do not need to be defeated by sinful thoughts.

All the tools discussed so far in this book, including our positive answer to Christ's big question, help to build what I call a Structurally Wise Life. I invite you to remember that term as we examine it more in depth in this chapter.

A structurally wise life helps us overcome our lapses in logic. When we create a structurally wise life, we are looking for something beyond a one-step solution, beyond our own willpower, something that overturns our inclinations to behave illogically. We construct various routines and practices that help us consistently avoid sin and choose Christ instead. These structures help us walk in step with the Holy Spirit and experience a new quality of life.

Think of the structures as if they were both the walls of a fort and the banks of a river. Walls shelter us and our loved ones and keep us safe. Banks enable flow and direction. The walls prevent the negative. The banks encourage the positive.

Once the structures are created, we can depend less upon our split-second decision-making and more upon a series of wise decisions we've laid in place ahead of time. Our life becomes governed not so much by momentary occurrences when our willpower might be depleted, but by the Holy Spirit's power working in us according to a series of wise decisions we've already committed to. We can avoid an extramarital affair, for instance, because we've previously decided many times in our mind never to entertain that possibility. Or we can choose to undertake a great ministry opportunity because we've already chosen many times in our mind to connect with Christ. We are spiritually awake and emotionally aware when there are needs to be met and services to be rendered out of reverence for Christ. Establishing a strong equity of faith brings glory to God because we are not as vulnerable to falling into temptation. The more we walk by faith, the more our minds are focused on Christ.

Creating protective structures works in conjunction with common sense. We don't linger in conversation with an office worker we admire. We move on. We don't share intimate details about our struggles at home. We keep our hearts safe. When a particular person's presence energizes us in questionable ways, if we feel a twinge of sexual chemistry, or if we realize that person occupies our thoughts and affects our feelings, then we are more careful about time spent with them, not less.

If you feel you are a long way from living a structurally wise life, there is hope for change and transformation. Romans 12:2 offers a time-tested truth and shows us the way minds are renewed and changed. In the previous verse, the Apostle Paul has urged us to offer our bodies as living sacrifices, holy and pleasing to God. Then he gives some strong encouragement in verse 2.

> Don't copy the behavior and customs of this world, but let God transform you into a new person by changing the way you think. Then you will learn to know God's will for you, which is good and pleasing and perfect. (NLT)

The instruction is laid out for us: "Let God transform you into a new person by changing the way you think." The benefit is also made clear. The more we are mentally tuned into God and His will, the more certain we are about His will for our life. We live in the path of His will as a confident, transformed person with a new quality of life.

The ultimate power to change lies with God. He does the transforming. Yet we have a responsibility in this process to agree with God, not to copy any harmful behaviors and customs of the world, and to welcome the change that He brings. We partner with Him by adopting an attitude of agreement and through various activities that help renew our minds. We partner with God in creating wise structures that help us keep in step with the Holy Spirit and facilitate the transformation.

Consider five time-tested, powerful, and practical ways that our thinking can be affected positively. Sometimes change can happen quickly, in a matter of hours. At other times, change will emerge over the long term. As we create these wise structures, we rely less on our moment-by-moment decision making and more on the overall structures to guide our life. The walls of the house keep us safe. The banks of the river let our life flow freely. These are ways to help retrain our brains toward godliness.

Let's look at each of these five in depth.

1. Regularly pray by using preset cues.

Have you ever been at church and seen somebody you know, but struggled to remember their name? The person walks up to you, sees the confusion on your face, and says, "Here's a hint: it starts with an H." Suddenly, you remember. Ham. Your friend was named after one of Noah's three sons. And also a delicious smoked meat.

The hint acted as a trigger that stirred your memory. Cue-oriented prayer is something we can undertake to help facilitate Christ's transformation. With this method, some of our prayers are deliberate, shorter, and tied to life's daily routines. It doesn't mean we don't also pray spontaneously or for longer periods of time. It means we also choose to pray sincerely at scattered intervals throughout each day, and that we automatically remember to pray by allowing certain events or people to trigger the prayer.

For instance, perhaps when we wake in the morning, we hit the alarm clock and choose to pray the words of Psalm 118:24. "This is the day that you have made, Lord. I'm going to rejoice and be glad in it." The prayer is sincere, and it's automatically built into our day. Hitting the alarm clock is our cue to begin the day focused on Christ.

After getting ready for work, we jump into our car for the commute. The opening of our car door is the next cue we have chosen as a reminder to pray another short prayer. "Lord Jesus, help all of my life to bring honor to you, including when and how I drive."

Perhaps next, we pass a business that has practices we don't agree with. The sign on the building acts as our cue to pray. Instead of railing against the business, we pray for the salvation of the people who run it, that their eyes would be opened to God's truth (Ephesians 1:18).

Maybe after we park, the door of our workplace itself becomes the next cue. We pray for the filling of God's Holy Spirit as we work today (Ephesians 5:18), and that we would do it all for the ultimate glory of the Lord (Colossians 3:23–24).

Throughout the remainder of the day, we continue to pray as the preset cues remind us. We can establish the cues any way we want. This helps us to "pray without ceasing" (1 Thessalonians 5:17). The constant prayer keeps our mind focused on Christ. In the instruction of Romans 12:2, we aren't copying the behavior and customs of this world, but we are letting God transform us into a new person by changing the way we think.

This can feel like a very different way of living if it's new to you. Before saying, "That's not who I am," or "That's way too extreme for me," consider this: These cues, prayers, and scriptures can be the path to a life of meaning, purpose, and freedom for you. Remember the phrase "I want to get well!" This is exactly what God wants for you, because it links you to Him and not the world. How about trying it for a day? A week? A month? Pretty soon, you'll find that you're enjoying a new quality of life. It's a life of truth, transformation, and prayer.

Can prayer cause literal changes to the brain? Yes. Researcher Dr. Andrew Newberg conducted an experiment on the effects of prayer using functional magnetic resonance imaging. Newberg's findings demonstrated actual quantifiable changes in brain volume and metabolism in people who prayed as little as twelve minutes per day.[1] Other studies have shown that intentionally meditating (or praying) for as little as thirty seconds can positively affect the brain.[2]

2. Keep worship music on autoplay.

Music has always been an important part of my life. I was a soloist in the Singing Cadets at Texas A&M and then majored in music at Baylor University. For two years, I was a minister of music at a church.

There are many types of Christian music, and they all help do one thing: put thoughts of God into your heart. Imagine your mind as a large auditorium. The music you play and sing fills the auditorium. I relish the practice of regularly praying the thoughts that

---

[1] Andrew Newberg and Mark Robert Waldman, *How God Changes Your Brain* (New York: Ballantine Books, 2010), 6–7.

[2] Dean Radin, "Testing Nonlocal Observation as a Source of Intuitive Knowledge," *EXPLORE: The Journal of Science and Healing* 4, no. 1 (January 2008): 23–35, https://doi.org/10.1016/j.explore.2007.11.001.

worship music brings into my mind. I want the thoughts of God in my brain even more than I want the melody.

Worship music is important because there's tremendous wisdom in continually exposing our thoughts to God's thoughts. Colossians 3:16 says, "Let the word of Christ dwell in you richly, teaching and admonishing one another in all wisdom, singing psalms and hymns and spiritual songs, with thankfulness in your hearts to God." If singing doesn't come naturally to you, listening to psalms and hymns and spiritual songs is the next best thing.

God knew exactly what He was talking about when He instructed the Apostle Paul to write that verse, because worship has been shown to have positive, literal, neurophysiological benefits. When we worship, we actually help heal our body and brains. Dr. Michael Liedke writes:

> Worship's effects on the amygdala have also been well studied and demonstrate a wide range of effects as a result of the hypoactivation or down-regulation to the fight or flight mechanism. The result is a significant decrease in the deleterious effects of chronic fight or flight activation and the decrease in heart rate, blood pressure, blood glucose levels, and serum markers of inflammation.
>
> This hypoactivation also has measurable psychic effects; measurable decreases in depression, anxiety, chronic pain, and even posttraumatic stress have been identified and can be traced back to one daily action, worship.
>
> These findings have been so robust that incorporating prayer (and worship) as part of the treatment plan for pathologies ranging from anxiety/depressive disorders,

hypertension, diabetes mellitus, and disorders of chronic inflammation has been encouraged.[3]

Whenever and wherever we worship, we revere God. We show devotion to Him. We keep our mind on Christ. We don't have to wait until Sunday to worship. We can worship in our car. We can worship at home. We can worship as we fall asleep at night. We can worship as we're hiking along a trail. We build the wise structure. Again, in the encouragement of Romans 12:2, we aren't copying the behavior and customs of this world, but we are letting God transform us into a new person by changing the way we think.

3. Continually set Scripture in front of your eyes.

I advocate regular and frequent biblical meditation—mentally dwelling on Scripture. Reading it and reading it again. Sometimes I'll read a specific passage ten times in a row. Or I'll read the same portion every day for a month. Many times, I'll pick a snippet of Scripture and dwell on it in my mind throughout the day.

Consider this: I've done some terribly shameful things in my life. Satan would love to drag out that old, abandoned shame and have me live there. On those days, I repeat over and over again a snippet of a verse that lifts the focus from my shame and places my focus on the God who took it away. Ephesians 2:4 says, "God is rich in mercy." I fill my thoughts with that powerful reminder. I might tell myself that fact a hundred times over the course of a day.

In days past, we advocated Bible memorization, which I still hold to strongly. But these days, I'm more cautious about instructing believers to memorize Scripture because people tend to tune out

---

[3] Michael Liedke, "Neurophysiological Benefits of Worship," *The Journal of Biblical Foundations of Faith and Learning* 3, no. 1 (2018), https://knowledge.e.southern.edu/jbffl/vol3/iss1/22.

when they hear it. Memorization seems too hard. It takes too much time—at least that's what they say.

To be clear, I greatly value Bible memorization. If you're willing to memorize, I suggest short passages at first. Write the verse down on a notecard. Place it in plain sight. If memorization seems too hard, remember that in the last chapter we looked at the benefits of Bible reading, particularly with an eye to rereading. That's what I emphasize in my instruction to people these days. Memorize if you can, but if you can't, just read Scripture, then reread it and reread it again. The memorization will happen as you continually ingest it. The Scripture will get lodged in your mind.

I recommend using any memory shortcuts you wish. Draw images of what you read. Write out passages in longhand. Read it aloud—anything to help you get Scripture into your mind and keep it there. It's not mindless repetition. We always want to read Scripture with sincerity and comprehension, with an eye to understand its meaning and to apply it to our lives. The point is this: God's truth is found in God's Word. Any way we can get it into our minds will be good for us.

Incidentally, I tend to keep a lot of open Bibles in my house. There's an open Bible on the coffee table. By my nightstand. On my desk in my home office. I deliberately keep the pages of the Bibles open. A closed Bible doesn't do any good. I've found that when a Bible is open, I am more apt to read it. When I find a verse that directly addresses what I'm going through, or that one of the kids is experiencing, I write out the verse on a sticky note and pin it next to my computer screen, on the front of the fridge, or on the bathroom mirror. I want Scripture always before my eyes. I want to read it when I'm not even trying to read it.

Perhaps there is no greater tool for retraining a brain than constant Bible exposure. As we saw, John 8:31–32 instructs us not only to know the teachings of Scripture but to "hold to" them. This means we "abide in his word" (ESV), or "continually obey [His] teachings and live in accordance with them" (AMP). It's not enough simply to give a head nod to the truth. We need to regularly place God's truth in our lives and dwell on it continually.

The ultimate benefit of biblical meditation doesn't come from the action. It comes from the power of God as we are in relationship with Him. Specifically, I counsel people to focus on Christ during biblical meditation and not to empty their minds, as is popular today. Dr. Timothy R. Jennings writes:

> Truth is comprehended via the left hemisphere of the brain, whereas our sense of unity, oneness, and relational connectedness is experienced in the right side of our brains.
>
> Biblical meditation, rather than focusing the mind on nothingness, emptying the mind, or chanting repetitive mantras, always focuses on some substantive aspect of God and his character of love.
>
> All through Scripture it is the same. God calls us to meditate on his law of love, which is an expression of his character of love. Such meditation requires the balanced engagement of both right and left hemispheres. Such balance not only results in greater health and peace but also growth in Christlikeness.[4]

4. Fast regularly.

Fasting is voluntarily reducing or eliminating the foods we eat for a set amount of time. We can fast from other things such as

---

[4] See Dr. Timothy Jennings, *The God-Shaped Brain*, expanded edition (Downers Grove, Illinois: IVP Books, 2017).

television, our phones, or even a relationship. And that can be good. Yet the specific type of fasting I'm recommending here is from food.

If you have any medical problems, I recommend checking with your doctor before fasting. Yet for most people, regular short-term fasting is an age-old practice that can effectively help reset a body's chemistry. It's one of the best ways I know to increase attentiveness to spiritual matters, lower stress, and help focus a mind on Christ.

Jesus fasted in the wilderness as part of His strategy to overcome temptation (Matthew 4:1–11). Ezra fasted and prayed for strength and safety (Ezra 8:21–23). The Israelites fasted to seek God's guidance (Judges 20:26). Queen Esther fasted together with all the Jews in Susa for vigilance and wisdom (Esther 4:16). Nehemiah fasted as part of his grieving process (Nehemiah 1:4). Fasting is shown as a means of expressing repentance and humility before the Lord (1 Samuel 7:6). The early disciples fasted and prayed before intensive ministry undertakings (Acts 13:3–4). Socrates said he fasted for mental clarity.[5]

As Thomas Ryan, a dedicated faster, once wrote:

> I fast to pull the loose ends together in my life. Since I've been fasting, I'm more sensitive to what messages are coming from both my heart and my body. About a year ago, I began fasting one day a week. It's been the most settled, healthy, productive year of my life.[6]

The biochemistry behind fasting shows its benefits. The pancreas rests. The blood pressure regulates. Stored sugar is burned up. Cravings cease. According to researchers,

---

[5] The Galen Foundation, "Fasting for Survival Lecture by Dr. Pradip Jamnadas," YouTube, August 16, 2019, https://www.youtube.com/watch?v=RuOvn4UqznU.

[6] Thomas Ryan, *Fasting Rediscovered* (New York: Paulist Press, 1981), 5.

> Fasting improves cognition, stalls age-related cognitive decline, usually slows neurodegeneration, reduces brain damage and enhances functional recovery after stroke, and mitigates the pathological and clinical features of epilepsy and multiple sclerosis in animal models.[7]

I know a man who dabbled in pornography off and on for years. He still feels cravings for it every so often and insists that one of the best ways he can control them is by fasting one day a week. The fasting brings him closer to the Lord and helps shift his mindset, and it also works on a physical level, helping calm his body and its cravings.

Another man in his early thirties was dating a woman who was working on her graduate degree in another city. They planned to get married, but due to his job and her schooling, they needed to be apart for two years. During that long season, they saw each other only one weekend per month. The man said he was finding it difficult physically to honor his girlfriend during the times when they were together, but then he began to fast. About the only way he felt "in control" during their times together was when he was regularly fasting. For most of those two years, he fasted every Tuesday and Thursday, and they were able to maintain their sexual integrity.

Fasting doesn't need to be difficult. I've had friends who have done forty-day fasts; I recommend studying the subject in depth before attempting it on that level. But for most people, a simple fast of skipping two meals a week is enough to bring noticeable benefits. Essentially, you fast from dinner one night until dinner the next

---

[7] Matthew C. L. Phillips, "Fasting as a Therapy in Neurological Disease," *Nutrients* 11, no. 10 (October 17, 2019), https://www.ncbi.nlm.nih.gov/pmc/articles/PMC6836141/.

day. On the first evening, after eating a normal meal, you skip any evening snacks. Then go to sleep. Then wake up and go about your day, skipping breakfast and lunch, making sure you drink water. You eat a regular meal at dinnertime. That's enough of a fast to produce a calming and more focused effect on the body.

The fasting is part of the wise structure you build. Again, in the instruction of Romans 12:2, you aren't copying the behavior and customs of this world, but you are letting God transform you into a new person by changing the way you think.

5. Limit sugar intake.

A woman went to a bakery shop once a month to meet with a friend. They would each eat a pastry or a large slice of cake. She noticed that after each of those meetings, she felt an increased temptation toward illicit thoughts. She wondered why.

It's because the stimulants we eat and our mental health are closely linked. When we eat too much sugar, the brain produces huge chemical surges. If too much of a stimulant is consumed, it can produce a high, followed by a low—which is where a poor thought-life can factor in. The body begins to crave illicit thoughts or behavior as a pick-me-up.

Nutritionist Liana Werner-Gray explains:

> It is impossible to ignore the science revealing the correlations between what we eat and our mental health. Food has a crucial impact on the brain, nervous system, and endocrine system.
>
> In general, a processed-food lifestyle is not one that will sustain you for a lifetime. It harms the brain—it's *neurotoxic*—and has been proven to cause anxiety and other health problems. These foods cause negative mood swings.

The most neurotoxic food on the planet is refined sugar, which includes white table sugar, brown sugar, corn syrup, sucrose, fructose, and high-fructose corn syrup. When you have low levels of serotonin in the brain, [the hormone that regulates mood] you crave sugar. While you may feel good during your five-minute sugar high, you quickly experience a crash, accompanied by anxiety.[8]

Sugar takes your body on an unhealthy rollercoaster ride. For consistently good mental health, the science is evident: be very careful about what you eat.[9] The careful eating is part of the wise structure you build. Again, in the instruction of Romans 12:2, you aren't copying the behavior and customs of this world, but you are letting God transform you into a new person by changing the way you think.

A New Way of Living

Our brains can adapt, change, and rewire for the better. As the brain is spiritually and literally renewed by thinking God-honoring thoughts and by the work that Christ does to transform us, it creates behavioral changes in our life. Neuroscientist Andrew Newberg

---

[8] Liana Werner-Gray, *Anxiety-Free with Food* (Carlsbad, California: Hay House, 2020), 33, 36, 101, 112.

[9] See, for instance: TED-Ed, "How Sugar Affects the Brain—Nicole Avena," You-Tube, January 7, 2014, https://www.youtube.com/watch?v=lEXBxijQREo; Lewis Howes, "Eat These Foods to Heal Your Body & Mind Today | Dr. Caroline Leaf," YouTube, June 28, 2021, https://www.youtube.com/watch?v=wXDWkx2jmeQ; Nicole Avena, Pedro Rada, and Bartley Hoebel, "Evidence for Sugar Addiction: Behavioral and Ceurochemical Effects of Intermittent Excessive Sugar Intake," *Neuroscience & Biobehavioral Reviews* 32, no. 1 (2008): 20–39, https://doi.org/10.1016/j.neubiorev.2007.04.019.

and therapist Mark Robert Waldman point to this spiritual and literal change of the brain. They write:

> Religious and spiritual contemplation changes your brain because it strengthens a unique neural circuit that specifically enhances social awareness and empathy while subduing destructive feelings and emotions.
>
> The underlying mechanism that allows these changes to occur relates to a unique quality known as neuroplasticity; the ability of the human brain to structurally arrange itself in response to a wide variety of positive and negative events.
>
> Advances in neuroscience have revolutionized the way we think about the brain. Rather than seeing it as an organ that slowly matures during the first two decades of life, then withers away as we age, scientists now look at the human brain as a constantly changing mass of activity.
>
> In mammals, dendrites—the thousands of tentacle-like receptors extending from one end of every neuron (or nerve cell)—rapidly grow and retreat in a period of a couple of weeks. In fact, recent evidence has shown that [some] neuronal changes can take place in literally a matter of hours.[10]

So let's rewrite this chapter's opening parable, creating a conversation that occurs two months after the man's first visit. Some of his changes occurred quite quickly. Others took a few weeks.

---

[10] Newberg and Waldman, *How God Changes Your Brain*, 14–15.

Within the parable, we're not trying to point to easy answers or be trite, as if people's problems are always tied up nicely in the end. We don't want to minimize serious problems or suggest that life is always cut and dried. Rather, we want to sincerely cast a vision of good things to come. Christ can definitely bring about real and lasting change. With God, there is always hope. So here's the continuation of our parable:

"Hey there," the man said to his counselor. "I'm so glad you could help. My life doesn't feel so chaotic or troubled anymore. The big purple bruises and welts are gone from my face. The headaches have stopped. No more cracked teeth. I haven't broken my nose lately."

"Hmmm," said the counselor. "Tell me what you're doing differently."

"Everything you instructed," the man said. "I started by convincing myself that no matter how good it felt to hit myself in the head with a hammer, I didn't want to do that anymore. Not at my core. I didn't want to stay stuck in destructive habits any longer. I truly wanted to change. I wanted to get well."

"Good," said the counselor. "Did you stop the hammer use right away?"

"Pretty soon," said the man. "At first I had these terrific cravings to bash my head in. But I built the wise structures into my life to keep my mind focused on God, allowing Him to change the way I think. These days, my mind is so filled with good things, I hardly ever crave my hammer anymore."

The counselor nodded. "So the plan is working."

The man grinned. "The old has gone. The new has come. When it comes to hitting myself in the face with a hammer, that harmful habit is a thing of the past."

Key Takeaways

- Thinking logically is important, but we don't always act logically. Even though we know something is harmful, that knowledge by itself doesn't have the power to change our life. We need something more than mere logic.

- In order to change, we must want to change. Our will comes into play. Christ asks every person a simple question: "Do you want to get well?" We must answer this question with "Yes, I want to get well!" then continually remind ourselves of this core desire that we have chosen.

- Part of the key to positive change lies in building a structurally wise life. We construct structures that help us keep our mind on Christ. He transforms our life as we keep our thoughts on Him. We can help our thought life through fasting, lowering or eliminating our sugar intake, memorizing Scripture, reading Bible passages repeatedly, meditating on biblical truths, listening to worship music, and praying throughout the day.

CHAPTER 8

When You Think about Sex

I t's been said that during the Victorian era, only one piece of advice was given to a betrothed woman regarding her wedding night: "Lie still and think of England." Historians doubt the accuracy of the phrase.[1] It was probably a satirical commentary on the epoch, yet it illustrates the trouble that emerges when sexuality encounters repression. Sexuality is maligned and subverted when it is cast entirely as something disagreeable—a burden to be borne or a sin to be avoided either in deed or in thought life.

Far better to think of sex as designed by God to be fun. Yes, I use that word deliberately: fun. In its original and ideal state, the Bible shows sexuality as meant for unity and pleasure between people in an exclusive relationship. Adam and Eve were naked and unashamed in the Garden of Eden, and God said it was good. Genesis 2:24 points to this original blueprint: "Therefore a man

---

[1] "Just Close Your Eyes and Think of England," Quote Investigator, https://quote-investigator.com/2014/09/30/empire/.

shall leave his father and his mother and hold fast to his wife, and they shall become one flesh." We are encouraged today to express our sexuality in the mode of that initial modeling—with joy in our hearts and freedom in our souls.

And, yes, the Bible actually welcomes us to *think* about sex. Sound surprising? It can be a game-changer to learn that the Bible invites us to think sexual thoughts that align with God's Word. We might have been taught that every sexual thought is wrong, but that's not what the Bible shows. The Bible calls us to meditate on the Word of God, and as such, we can study with permission and encouragement any number of passages that deal with sexuality.

So, what might God-honoring sexual thoughts look like?

Biblical Sexual Thoughts

We need to start with 2 Timothy 3:16–17: "All Scripture is God-breathed and is useful for teaching, rebuking, and training in righteousness, so that the servant of God may be thoroughly equipped for every good work."

The big question, based on the passage, is how much of the Bible is useful? Read the passage again if needed. The word to remember comes right at the front.

All.

All scripture is useful.[2] It's that simple. We must let that truth permeate our minds. The Apostle Paul states emphatically that every bit of the Bible is inspired by God, completely trustworthy, important, and useful. Even the strange stories in Ezekiel. Even the dry lists of genealogies. Even the mysterious prophecies in Revelation. There's not one portion of the Bible that's not beneficial.

---

[2] *Strong's Greek Lexicon*, (G3956) "pas," Blue Letter Bible, https://www.blueletterbible.org/lexicon/g3956/kjv/tr/0-1/. The Greek word for "all" means all, whole, or entire.

Scripture never says, "Don't think about sex." Rather, through passage after passage, the Holy Spirit invites us to think God-honoring thoughts about sex. These thoughts fall into roughly three categories, although the placement of certain stories and teachings is debated. The categories are these:

1. God's perfect plan for sex.

God's perfect plan is displayed in passages such as Genesis 1 and 2, where sexuality is shown in its original design to be pure, undefiled, and amazing. Humans are made in the image of God, stamped with His approval as His representatives and agents in the world,[3] instructed to "be fruitful and multiply" (Genesis 1:26–28), and to enjoy the one-flesh relationship brought about by love-making (Genesis 2:24). Jesus later endorsed this blueprint in Matthew 19:4–6.

The perfect plan is noted in other passages such as Proverbs 5:18–19, where a husband is instructed to "rejoice in the wife of your youth; let her breasts fill you at all times with delight." And in 1 Corinthians 7:3–5, where husbands and wives are encouraged to have sex regularly.

When it comes to our thought life, some thinking about sexuality falls into this category of "perfect." This kind of thinking is welcomed and encouraged by God.

2. God's prohibitive plan for sex.

God's prohibitive plan shows boundaries that need to surround sexuality for our own good.

For instance, in Exodus 20:14, God clearly prohibits adultery. The psalmist declares, "I will not look with approval on anything

---

[3] Pete Enns, "What Does 'Image of God' Mean?," BioLogos, July 27, 2010, https://biologos.org/articles/what-does-image-of-god-mean/.

that is vile" (Psalm 103:3). Proverbs 23:27–28 strongly warns against sex with prostitutes. First Corinthians 6:13 says, "The body is not meant for sexual immorality but for the Lord."

Stories about the misuse of sexuality are also shown. For example, in 2 Samuel 13, King David's son, Amnon, rapes his sister, Tamar. This horrific crime produces in its wake a desolate woman, a furious half-brother, and ultimately a fratricide fueled by revenge.

When it comes to our thought life, some thinking about sexuality falls into the category of "prohibited." The activity or thoughts are dangerous and can bring harm. Our call is to agree with God that harmful is harmful and to respect His boundaries.

3. God's permissive plan for sex.

The word "permissive" in this sense doesn't equal God's approval. Rather, "permission" signifies God's allowance. Some choices that people make pass through God's permissive will, although these choices fall short of His perfect plan.

God allows people to freely choose their own actions and attitudes and go their own directions. Often in Scripture, God shows the consequences of these free choices, yet He still is able to redeem the experience for His own purposes. These choices play out within specific eras of history when different sexual norms were common within society, yet were not part of God's perfect plan.

For instance, during the era of the patriarchs, polygamy was culturally permitted. It wasn't part of God's perfect plan for Jacob to have two wives and two concubines. In fact, God shows the jealousy and infighting that happened within Jacob's family as a result. Yet God ultimately redeemed the experience and built the twelve tribes of Israel through the arrangement.

With our thought life, some thinking about sexuality falls into the category of "permissive." Perhaps the activity or thought is permitted, even fully accepted, by our culture, but it may or may not align with God's Word. Here, the warnings of Paul come into play: "'I have the right to do anything,' you say—but not everything is beneficial" (1 Corinthians 10:23a). Even though our culture says certain sexual activities are okay, the activities may not be beneficial for us.

Discernment is important. We must always live in alignment with God's truth. When Scripture does not speak directly to an issue, we need to live—and think—wisely.

Silver Towers and Paneled Cedar

It can be mind-blowing to realize that an entire book of the Bible is devoted to sexuality. The Song of Solomon, an explicit yet tastefully presented love poem, speaks frankly of breasts like twin fawns of a gazelle, kisses sweeter than wine, and the joy of sexual fulfillment. In the avenue of thinking God-honoring thoughts about sexuality, reading and even meditating on the book of Song of Solomon is a prime place to start. Keep in mind 2 Timothy 3:16–17— *all* Scripture is useful.

Some people wonder what the Song of Solomon is doing in the Bible. Well-meaning Bible teachers throughout time have tried to pass it off solely as an allegory of Christ's love for the Church. Others have taken the other extreme and contended that it's solely a sex manual. The legendary Charles Spurgeon (1834–1892) preached at least sixty-four sermons on the Song of Solomon, tactfully and beautifully mingling the approaches.[4] I side with Spurgeon and take the "both-and" approach.

---

[4] Charles Spurgeon, *Charles Spurgeon on the Song of Solomon: 64 Sermons to Ignite a Passion for Jesus!* (Christian Classics Treasury, 2013), Kindle.

When trying to grasp the intensity and devotion of Christ's love for the Church, it's hard to get our minds around that idea, so the Bible offers a picture of devoted love in the Song of Solomon. God loves us so fervently, so strongly, that it's the same sort of fervency and strength shown by spouses in an ideal marriage. Paul, in Ephesians 5:25–31, points to this comparison overtly. "Husbands, love your wives, just as Christ loved the church and gave himself up for her.... This is a profound mystery—but I am talking about Christ and the Church."

Pastor Aaron Menikoff writes:

> The Song of Songs really does point forward to Christ. As the wife longs to be with her husband (1:4; 3:1–4), so the Christian longs to be with Christ (Phil. 1:23).
>
> As the husband woos his wife with words (4:1–16; Ephesians 5:26), so Christ woos us with his Word (John 10:27).
>
> The love of a husband and wife is to be indelible (8:7). So, too, nothing can separate us from the love of Christ Jesus our Lord (Romans 8:37–39).[5]

Although the Song of Solomon can be taken allegorically, it also must be taken literally, because that's how the Bible is presented—except when it's clearly not literal. For instance, in John 6:35, Jesus says, "I am the bread of life." We see plainly that this is metaphoric language. Jesus walked and talked and lived as a real human being—not a big loaf of pumpernickel. Jesus goes on in the same verse to describe what He means: "Whoever comes to me

---

[5] Aaron Menikoff, "3 Reasons You Should Preach through the Song of Solomon," 9Marks, https://www.9marks.org/article/songofsongs/.

will never be hungry again." The clear symbolic language prevents a literal interpretation of the passage.

The Song of Solomon's literalness shines. The book presents and celebrates erotic love. Dr. Jay Harvey notes this, yet he also surfaces the challenges of our day when taking the book at face value. Sexuality can be tainted, which is why people get confused about the presence, content, and descriptiveness of the Song of Solomon. He writes:

> Sexual imagery is powerful. Our culture abounds with images and paradigms that corrupt more than they instruct and wound more than they heal. So much of the culture's presentation of sexuality is crass, lacking the beauty and mystery that should characterize the physical consummation and enduring love of marriage. A study of the Song of Solomon can revise our understanding and help us reclaim in holiness the sexual expression that God has created and declared good.
>
> This inspired poem encourages husbands and wives to share their adoration for each other with joy. The Song of Solomon contains sexual imagery in parts and is full of declarations of love and adoration. But the language is tasteful, poetic, and beautiful. It is ancient, divinely inspired language from another time. We need the fresh perspective on love and sexuality that the Song of Solomon offers.[6]

Without doing a full exposition of the book here and now, let's consider three important principles for pondering the sexuality presented in the Song of Solomon.

---

[6] Jay Harvey, "Why Study the Book of Song of Solomon?," Crossway, June 8, 2018, https://www.crossway.org/articles/why-study-the-book-of-song-of-solomon/.

1. All of Scripture agrees with all of Scripture.

We know "it is impossible for God to lie" (Hebrews 6:18), that God does not sin (2 Corinthians 5:21), and that all of the Bible came from the mind of the Holy Spirit (2 Timothy 3:16–17). So God wouldn't tell people that illicit sex is wrong in one part of the Bible, but good in another. The principle is this: All of Scripture agrees with all of Scripture. The Song of Solomon always needs to be seen in the full context of the entire Bible.

As such, the Song of Solomon is a God-honoring book, full of holy imagery. It is not included in the Bible to incite lust or any kind of impurity. Rather, it's given to teach and train us in righteousness. Sexuality is part of that righteousness. It's easy to look at any one passage of the Bible—in the Song of Solomon or elsewhere—and take it out of context. Yet note that all of the Song of Solomon always agrees with Ephesians 5:3: "Among you there must not be even a hint of sexual immorality, or of any kind of impurity, or of greed, because these are improper for God's holy people."

Two of the trickiest passages to interpret are Song of Solomon 3:1–4 and 5:6–7. In the first section, the female speaker searches the streets for the one she loves. When she finally finds him, she brings him back to her mother's house and holds tightly to him, expressing the intensity of her feelings. In 5:6–7, the male speaker knocks on the door of his lover's abode, intent upon making love, or so runs the implication. He leaves before she answers the door; she searches for him, but does not find him.

We must ask: If these two lovers are married, why are they not living in the same house? Or, if they are not married, why is the intent of sexual activity presented so fervently between them? The answers must align with Ephesians 5:3. Perhaps this story is being told in a spirit of warning: They have awakened love too soon, so they need to be careful and progress toward marriage quickly. Or perhaps the story is of two married people being kept apart and of the intense longing they feel toward each other. It's difficult to draw a conclusion. Yet we know for sure that Song of Solomon 3:1–4 and 5:6–7 are not endorsing sexual activity outside of marriage, because all of Scripture agrees with all of Scripture.

2. The story in Song of Solomon isn't presented sequentially.

Nonsequential storytelling was a commonly used technique within ancient poetry. The storyline of the Song of Solomon is not presented sequentially, and in a casual reading, you might wonder who's doing the speaking or what stage of relationship the two people are at—if they're married or not. Some scholars think the Song of Solomon might not present a single love story, but rather several stories or poems all at once.[7]

Think of the nonlinear structure of the book like this: In most of the stories we are familiar with in modern Western culture, a story progresses in a straight line. We start at the beginning with "Once upon a time" and progress to the finish with "they all lived happily ever after." The plot points progress like this: A B C D E F G...

But in ancient times, you looked at a story the way you would look at a painting on a wall. You might glance at the righthand upper corner, then the lefthand lower corner, then the middle. The whole painting was understood as one image with many facets. In nonlinear storytelling, the sequence of events could be presented like a swirl of paint on a canvas, like this:

B D
C A E F
G

---

[7] Gordon H. Johnston, "14 Reasons Why Song of Solomon Probably Doesn't Tell a Single Love Story," DTS Voice, February 14, 2015, https://voice.dts.edu/article/song-of-solomon-love-story-or-love-stories-gordon-h-johnston/.

Dr. Douglas O'Donnell explains:

> The Song is a song, but also a minidrama that contains refrains, bodily descriptions, dream sequences, and a climactic definition of love. The full story of the bride and groom is far from complete. No names, specific locations, or aspects of their courtship are provided, but there is enough of a storyline to decipher the drama. The Song tells the love story of a young couple who, with the blessing of friends and family, celebrates their commitment and consummation.
>
> The shape of that story is debated. Some scholars believe the couple moves from courtship to the wedding to married life. Other scholars, due to the physical forthrightness of the first lines, set the whole Song within the context of marriage.[8]

3. Song of Solomon encourages us to be neither walls nor doors.
Our third principle addresses a large-scale theme of sexuality for us to think about and live by. A clear takeaway is found at the end of the book. In Song of Solomon 8:8–9, the friends of the lovers take up the song. They describe how they have a little sister, "too young for breasts," and they wonder aloud what they will do to help her when she is ready for marriage. They conclude:

> If she is a wall,
>   we will build towers of silver on her.
> If she is a door,
>   we will enclose her with panels of cedar.

---

[8] Douglas O'Donnell, "Song of Solomon: A Commentary," The Gospel Coalition, https://www.thegospelcoalition.org/commentary/song-of-solomon/.

A "wall" means she is unyielding and immovable, closed to sexual advances. A "door" is poetic language implying that she swings open freely. The friends don't want her to err toward either imbalance. They don't want her to be a prude, and they don't want her to be a tramp. Or, stated positively: They want her to enjoy all that sexual love has to offer, but they want her to do so within boundaries. They want her to have both the towers of silver on the wall and the panels of cedar that safeguard the door. And there's our principle for sexual thinking: full enjoyment but respect of boundaries.

As one of the female friends explains in the next verse, Song of Solomon 8:10,

> I am a wall,
>   and my breasts are like towers.
> Thus I have become in his eyes
>   like one bringing contentment.

That's a mindset we can all adopt. When it comes to our sexuality, including our thought life, we are to be neither a wall nor a door. We are to be neither prudish nor licentious. We are invited to relish our sexuality, yet to do so within God-honoring boundaries. We are called to live with the joys of silver towers as well as the safeguards of paneled cedar. To put it in a short memorable phrase: *My sexual thoughts don't run wild*. Yes, I have God-honoring sexual thoughts, but no, they are not uncontrolled.

In sum, the Song of Solomon shows the physical display of affection as expressed purely in marriage. Since Song of Solomon is Scripture, and all Scripture is beneficial, it is therefore "useful for teaching, rebuking, correcting and training in righteousness" (2 Timothy 3:16).

One important caution: Before you read or meditate upon the Song of Solomon, ask yourself some hard questions. You might have been exposed to a lot of pornography, and as such it may be difficult for you to separate what you have seen from the imagery presented in the Song of Solomon. If this is the case, be careful not to impose lies upon the truth of this biblical book.

In the Song of Solomon, the sexuality is shown from the perspective of tenderness, mutuality, kindness, commitment, responsibility, and genuine love. The lover and the beloved display their affection for one another in caring and honoring ways. By contrast, in pornography, people interact with each other solely to gratify their lusts. People are used, maligned, hurt, shamed, imposed upon, objectified, and ignored or frightened. If you have immersed yourself in that world, then you may have been indoctrinated into falsely believing that's what all sex should be like. You may have some unlearning to do before you can grasp the words and imagery of the Song of Solomon.

If in doubt about reading the Song of Solomon, talk to your pastor or a counselor first.

A Difficult Yet Important Conversation

Any book about thought life and its implications for sexuality would not be complete without addressing self-stimulation. Specifically: If a Christian engages in this practice, what might that person think about while doing so? We need to examine this topic carefully, forthrightly, and with biblical understanding. I realize this topic can make people uncomfortable. Yet if the Church does not address this, who will? We don't want to relegate this subject to the media, backstreets, and underbelly of our culture.

In today's secular culture, masturbation is usually seen as "benign and healthy."[9] Yet, for a believer, the practice is not as straightforward. Even to reach the big question, we must discuss some foundational questions first, because the Bible is largely silent on self-stimulation. The Bible doesn't condemn masturbation, but it doesn't make overt allowances for it either. Since the Bible is largely silent, we need to use biblical discernment to address this issue. We must see what passages might relate to this subject, then draw careful conclusions.

The "Onan" Question

Recently, a woman spoke with me at a NewLife Marriage weekend. She was highly upset that we did not call masturbation a sin, and she was adamant that the Bible states it's an abomination. She pointed to Genesis 38:8–10, where Onan "spilled his semen on the ground." Verse 10 reads: "What he did was wicked in the LORD's sight; so the LORD put him to death." She is not alone in this belief.

Yet a closer reading of that text shows that Onan was put to death because he refused to fulfill the totality of a levirate marriage—that is, he didn't marry the wife of his deceased brother and produce an heir, which was God's specific command for that culture in Deuteronomy 25:5–10. Under Mosaic law, any children produced by such a union were considered the offspring of the deceased husband, and as such, they were entitled to all privileges of that estate.

Onan was objectifying his brother's widow and using her for his own gratification. He was not fulfilling his duty to her as prescribed

---

[9] Hugo Schwyzer, "Masturbation Is at the Root of the Culture Wars," *The Atlantic,* May 22, 2013, https://www.theatlantic.com/sexes/archive/2013/05/masturbation-is-at-the-root-of-the-culture-wars/276110.

by Mosaic law. Correctly interpreted, the passage cannot be used to denounce masturbation. Even so, I don't dismiss the story of Onan entirely when it comes to sexual practices for today. The larger point of the story is that sexuality and responsibility must go together. That's a truth for any time.

The Leviticus Question

Some biblical scholars make allowances for self-stimulation based on Leviticus 15:16–18. Here, God is revealing cultural patterns for his nation, and he goes into explicit detail. The Holy Spirit through Moses states that after a man's semen is expelled, the only requirement is bathing.

Some Christians insist that the passage deals solely with ejaculation during intercourse, but the text makes an important distinction between verses 16–17 and verse 18. Verses 16–17 relate to a general release of semen, and only a man is instructed to bathe. By comparison, verse 18 mentions an emission during intercourse, and here, both the man and the woman are instructed to bathe.

In both mentions, no condemnation is given for the release of semen. So, verses 16–17 could be referring to a release of semen due to a nocturnal emission, or the passage could make an allowance for a release due to self-stimulation.

Interestingly, a man is deemed "unclean" in this passage after he releases semen, and due to the use of that word, some Christians conclude that "unclean" is the same as sin. But that's not what the text shows. In the verses that immediately follow, a woman is considered "unclean" when she has her period (Leviticus 15:19–20). The same Hebrew word is used in both instances—for the release of semen and for menstruation. It's certainly not a sin for a woman to have her period, so we know that the use of "unclean" for the release of semen is a cleanliness issue only.

The "Apostle Paul" Question

Some Christians point out that when married people take a break from sex, the solution for sexual tension that Paul offers is prayer—not self-stimulation. They note Paul's teaching for married couples in 1 Corinthians 7:5: "Do not deprive each other except perhaps by mutual consent and for a time, so that you may devote yourselves to prayer. Then come together again so that Satan will not tempt you because of your lack of self-control."

I agree with this observation. This would have been a prime place for Paul to provide an overt endorsement for masturbation, but he didn't. All he said to do was to devote more time to prayer. So, by not mentioning masturbation, several questions are raised:

- Was Paul erring on the side of decorum? For whatever reason, perhaps he did not want to address this subject. He wanted to emphasize prayer and put that into people's minds as most important.
- Or was he giving an all-encompassing directive? Perhaps he was saying that prayer is all that's acceptable, period.
- Or was he merely being concise without providing a full list of legitimate options? When married people deprive themselves, it's okay to take a cold shower or go for a run—but Paul didn't mention those things either.

The text doesn't provide the fuller answer. So it's problematic to use this passage as a prooftext to condemn masturbation. To produce a blanket condemnation is an argument from silence, an incomplete answer at best.

Three Main Approaches

When it comes to self-stimulation, the Bible gives us many commands that relate to sexuality in general. We need to avoid lust (Matthew 5:28), live with self-control (Titus 2:11–12), avoid sexual immorality (1 Thessalonians 4:3–5), honor married sex (Hebrews 13:4), and avoid "even a hint of sexual immorality, or of any kind of impurity" (Ephesians 5:3). As believers, we always need to carefully live in step with the Holy Spirit and run in the pathways of God's commands. None of these commands specifically address self-stimulation, but we can deduce, again, that boundaries and sexuality go hand in hand.

Christian leaders and scholars carefully sift through the previously mentioned passages and offer a variety of approaches to the subject. The main three stances are these,[10] although variations exist on each:

1. Always wrong, all the time.

First, some Christian leaders and scholars equate all masturbation with sin, or at least insist that self-stimulation misses the point when it comes to sexuality. Ultimately, they condemn the activity, contending that masturbation cannot be mentally separated from lust.

They may additionally take a strong position on the design argument, believing that the act of solo sex circumvents God's model for married sex. Since masturbation doesn't aid marital bonding, it falls outside permissible boundaries established by God, they say.

I'm mindful that some orthodox churches, synods, and denominations put forward the "always wrong, all the time" stance for all their followers or congregants.

---

[10] See James M. Rochford, "Biblical Ethics of Masturbation," Evidence Unseen, https://www.evidenceunseen.com/theology/practical-theology/biblical-ethics-of-masturbation/.

2. Normal, natural, and to be encouraged.

The second stance, taken by other Christian leaders and scholars, is that self-stimulation is permissible and healthy. As long as the lust and self-control issues are dealt with, solo sex can be enjoyed on a sensation-only basis, or if a person is thinking about their current, future, or former spouse (i.e., if a spouse has died).

They contend that self-stimulation helps prevent premarital sex for single people. It keeps married people away from affairs. Medically, it slightly lowers the odds of prostate cancer and offers other health benefits.[11]

They offer few, if any, prohibitions and encourage Christians in this direction as a normal and natural part of life.

3. Sometimes helpful, sometimes harmful.

The third approach, favored by other Christian leaders and scholars, is that the activity of self-stimulation falls somewhere between the first and second stances. Scripture doesn't prohibit it, so for us to do so would position us dangerously close to legalism. Yet, since the practice may lead to illicit thinking or a lack of self-control, they don't place a blanket endorsement on it, either.

Bible teacher Paul Byerly writes:

> Is there any other sexual sin that is not directly and clearly identified as sin in the Bible? There are passages which clearly label as sin such things as fornication, adultery, lust, incest, rape, [illicit] homosexuality, and even bestiality.

---

[11] Scott Gottlieb, "Frequent Ejaculation May Be Linked to Decreased Risk of Prostate Cancer," *British Medical Journal* 328, no. 7444 (April 10, 2004): 851, https://www.ncbi.nlm.nih.gov/pmc/articles/PMC387502/.

> Surely the urge to masturbate is more common than most of these and much stronger than many of them, yet the Bible says nothing about it. If God felt it necessary to tell us not to have sex with animals, why didn't He also find it necessary to tell us not to masturbate?[12]

Byerly makes a strong point, as long as we don't extrapolate his teaching and conclude that anything and everything that's not specifically prohibited in the Bible is acceptable.

While there is no definitive biblical prohibition against masturbation, there are some circumstances that make it sinful or harmful, and some circumstances where it may be okay—which brings us to the big question.

The Big Question

If a believer self-stimulates, what might that person think about while doing so? With the foundational issues now addressed and the approaches now understood, let's tackle that big question, particularly for those who hold to the second or third approaches. Let's look at some clear boundaries first, and then at potential freedoms.

Boundaries

Based on biblical passages that pertain to general sexuality, we can conclude that if we are married, it is a break of fidelity and therefore immoral to sexually fantasize about anyone who is not our spouse. If we are single, it is immoral to mentally lust after

---

[12] Paul Byerly, "Why Didn't God Call It Sin?," The Marriage Bed, https://themarriagebed.com/why-didnt-god-call-it-sin/.

someone we are not married to, whether the person being fantasized about is married or single (Matthew 5:27–28).

Unquestionably, it is sinful to masturbate using pornography, which degrades and demeans people. This includes mental pornography, as well as visual, audible, or readable pornography.

Incidentally, I've been involved in addictions counseling for more than four decades, and when we work with a person recovering from sexual addictions (including compulsive pornography use), we recommend that the person abstain from masturbation forever.

To put that advice into another framework, a healthy Christian might be able to walk into a bar or drink a glass of wine and experience no problems. But if that Christian is an alcoholic in recovery, then we recommend a plan that includes complete abstinence from alcohol as part of the path that leads toward healing and restoration. The alcoholic in recovery must not drink socially or even walk into a bar.

Similarly, when it comes to someone who is in recovery from sexual addictions, masturbation and pornography have become too closely associated. The act of masturbation and the compulsions that trigger the addiction are too closely linked. There can be no masturbation for a person recovering from sexual addictions.

Potential Freedoms

For married people in normative and nonaddictive situations, the three-part standard to espouse is this: Everything sexual in your life needs to 1) be known by your spouse, 2) be approved by your spouse, 3) mentally involve your spouse. Meaning: a married person's mind needs to be solely focused on the spouse during any sexual activity—whether intercourse or self-stimulation.

Certainly, when spouses are making love, self-stimulation can be an acceptable part of their intimacy together. Couples don't always experience simultaneous orgasms. In these cases, self-stimulation is not an isolated, detached act. It can be part of a mutually satisfying sexual experience.

Another allowance might be for extended travel. For instance, a husband or wife might be stationed overseas for a year in the military. If they are both aware of their respective activities, approve of them, and mentally involve each other, then their self-stimulation is most likely acceptable. It could be a way for them to stay more deeply connected.

A person in a marriage where one person is infirm or physically unable to have intercourse might self-stimulate in the welcomed presence of their spouse or by imagining their spouse. For both parties, the theme of 1 Corinthians 13:7–8 NASB may take precedent: "Love... believes all things, hopes all things, endures all things. Love never fails."

For single Christians, the answer is more intricate. Some Christian leaders contend that self-stimulation is indeed possible without succumbing to immoral thoughts. One option for single people might be to adopt a mindset focused solely on bodily sensation.

God designed people's bodies to experience pleasure—all sorts of pleasure, including sexual. It's okay to enjoy the sensation of a hot shower on your shoulders or the delight of eating your favorite food. No fantasy life is needed for these God-given pleasures—or perhaps for self-stimulation also. As Bible teacher Simone Samuels writes,

> One of the main arguments I hear against masturbation
> [is that] masturbation is based on lust. Many times yes,

but not necessarily. It is possible to masturbate and even
orgasm without lusting after someone, without any sort
of fantasy.[13]

Another option for single people, although not without controversy, is that a mindset focused on marriage can be God-
honoring—even for single people who self-stimulate. In this case,
the principle of Hebrews 13:4 applies: "Marriage should be honored by all, and the marriage bed kept pure."

As such, a single person might focus on the imagery of an
unspecific person they will one day marry. They mentally acknowledge before God their fidelity to their future spouse. Or a divorced
person who is not remarried might envision the ideal potential of
their former spouse. Or they might picture an unspecific new mate
God has in waiting. For a person who believes they will never
marry, or if they have the gift of singleness, perhaps the focus is
the unspecific spouse that might have been, or the spouse that God
might have given if they didn't have the gift. Faces and names are
deliberately kept ambiguous. The mental category of "spouse" is
kept in the forefront.

I realize we are in debatable territory, and I hope this chapter
creates a healthy overall discussion about this subject within the
Church. I am not attempting to put any illicit images into anyone's
head, and please note that it is certainly okay for any person not
to masturbate.

Rather, I am seeking to present categories where the Holy
Spirit can guide believers into all truth. I pray that you will trust
the Holy Spirit to show you what is helpful and not harmful, to

---

[13] Simone Samuels, "Is Masturbation a Sin?," *Simone Samuels* (blog), June 15, 2018,
https://simonesamuels.wordpress.com/2018/06/15/is-masturbation-a-sin/.

reveal lines you must not cross, and ultimately to lead you into all righteousness—in your sexual life, as well as in every other aspect of life. As believers, we can have sexual thoughts, but they can't run wild.

A God-Honoring Sexual Thought Life

The Bible indicates that some practices and beliefs indeed don't come with clear-cut teaching, and that certain issues are left up to the consciences of individual believers.[14] Romans 14:5 offers a prime example of how to deal with a disputable matter: One person considers one day more sacred than another; another considers every day alike. Each of them should be fully convinced in their own mind.

The issues presented in this chapter are open to honest dialogue, and I encourage all of us in the faith-based community to respect and not malign the Christians with whom we don't agree.[15] It can be easy to hear that Pastor Smith from the First Church on the Corner teaches a particular stance that we don't agree with, so we condemn Pastor Smith and label him and his congregation as heretics. This needs to stop. Rather, on issues of secondary importance, we need to respect that Pastor Smith has studied the issue and holds a different opinion. Our responsibility is further study of our own careful listening and robust discussion. Condemning each other benefits no one.

Overall in this chapter, I want to underscore that it is okay for believers to think God-honoring sexual thoughts. Not every

---

[14] See D. A. Carson, "On Disputable Matters," *Themelios* 40, no. 3, https://www.thegospelcoalition.org/themelios/article/on-disputable-matters/.

[15] For two opposing viewpoints, see Michael Moore and Karsten Kaczmar, "Embracing Controversy: Christians and Masturbation," Christians Who Curse Sometimes, September 29, 2021, https://christianswhocursesometimes.com/embracing-controversy-christians-and-masturbation/.

thought that enters our minds about sex is wrong or destructive, and if that is what we have been taught—by parents, churches, books, seminars, or parachurch organizations—then we need to turn away from lies and fill our minds with truth.

The Bible encourages us to express our sexuality with joy in our hearts, freedom in our souls, and integrity in our minds. We are to be neither prudish nor licentious. We are called to live with the joys of silver towers as well as the safeguards of paneled cedar.

Ultimately, we are invited to align all our thoughts—sexual or otherwise—with Philippians 4:8: "Whatever is true, whatever is noble, whatever is right, whatever is pure, whatever is lovely, whatever is admirable—if anything is excellent or praiseworthy—think about such things." When this happens, we honor God and enjoy a greater quality of life.

Key Takeaways

- Not every thought about sex that enters our mind is wrong. In fact, the Bible actually welcomes us to think sexual thoughts that align with God's Word. Some of our thoughts will align with God's original design for sexuality. Other thoughts will align with His prohibitions concerning sexuality—i.e., we will agree with God that harmful activity is harmful. And some of our thoughts will recognize that a culture permits certain sexual activities, but they may or may not be beneficial.
- An entire book in the Bible—the Song of Solomon—pertains to sexuality. According to 2 Timothy 3:16–17, "All Scripture is...useful," which means the Song of Solomon is useful, too. Keep in mind

when you read it that all of Scripture agrees with all of Scripture, the stories presented in the book aren't presented sequentially, and that the overall takeaway is that we are to be neither prudish nor licentious in our sexuality.

- Self-stimulation is neither explicitly forbidden nor championed in Scripture. Some believers choose to self-stimulate. Not all Christian scholars agree on the issue. A biblical case can be made that self-stimulation is sinful in some instances, yet it might be acceptable in other instances.

CHAPTER 9

Tend Your Garden

My first job was tending a garden. It was actually a cottonfield owned by Texas A&M University where research was being conducted to create nontoxic seeds that could be eaten like nuts. I learned a lot about growing plants from that season of my life. If you want a successful garden, you've got to do a lot more than sow the seeds and water them. Whenever I see a beautiful garden today, I know it's the result of a dedicated gardener and some genuine diligence.

To garden effectively, you need to stir up and slice the soil, dislodging weeds and tossing them aside, cultivating the ground one row after another. You spade one row then go on to the next. When the day turns warm, sweat beads on your forehead and back. The work is not necessarily easy. Your mind might be on the future bumper crop you hope will result—bushels of sun-sweetened tomatoes; rows of crunchy corn, hot and buttered on the table; fresh carrots; cucumbers; and squash.

Those who garden know that soil requires constant attention. If a garden is left unattended, it grows wild. Thistles and crabgrass overtake the soil. The ground becomes unproductive and hard. Rather, each springtime, gardens must be prepared and planted. Each summertime, they must be weeded and watered. Each autumn, they must be composted, rooted, and raked. Even in winter, the act of letting a garden lie fallow requires intentionality. For a garden to produce its greatest yield, it must be allowed to rest.

St. Francis of Assisi (1181–1226) knew about the constant attention gardens need to flourish. As the story is told, he was out hoeing his garden one day when a man walked up to him and called over the fence, "Brother! If you discovered you were going to die today before sunset, what would you be doing right now?"

We can hear the negative implications in the question. *You're wasting time, Francis. Surely, this is a lousy way to spend your day. You should be concerning yourself with eternal matters. A Christian of your position needs to live more urgently.*

We don't know the tone with which St. Francis responded—if with righteous indignation, or with a smile on his face. We do know that he died early, when he was only forty-four, so he wasn't aged and full of weariness when this question was posed. It wasn't that he was gardening because he had nothing else to do. In his few short years, he led an extremely productive and contemplative life, filled with teaching, writing, counseling, traveling, praying, worshipping, helping the poor, championing justice, and founding three monastic orders.

Evidently, gardening was also an important part of his life. He understood he could be fully in the will of God while attending to necessary routine matters, because we know how the friar replied to the question, "If you discovered you were going to die today before sunset, what would you be doing right now?"

St. Francis said: "I would finish hoeing my garden."

Constant Cultivation

We've discussed a lot of ideas in this book. Some you'll be able to recall instantly and apply to your life whenever needed. Others will need to be studied again before they become second nature. These will require reflection, perhaps with a journal and a Bible, or perhaps by discussing them with a group of trusted friends. Yet I want to leave you with one main idea:

You have to tend your garden.

When it comes to your thought life, grab the rake. Bring the watering can. Commit to constantly cultivating your mind. The phrase "You have to tend your garden" isn't original to me, and it's not original to St. Francis either, although he might have been the inspiration for it. The phrase actually comes from the novel *Candide*, written by the famous French philosopher Voltaire (1694–1778).[1]

Voltaire didn't hold to an orthodox Christian faith, but he embraced truth on many matters. In his worldview, tending a garden prevented a person from succumbing to what he viewed as the three great evils of this world: disillusionment, vice, and want. It also prevented a person from engaging in matters that might result in turmoil or destruction. He saw the solution to life's ills as

---

[1] For an interesting essay on Voltaire's use of the phrase "Tend our own gardens," see "What Voltaire Meant by 'One Must Cultivate One's Own Garden,'" The School of Life, https://www.theschooloflife.com/thebookoflife/cultivate-own-garden-voltaire.

a type of horticultural quietism. According to him, focusing on constant garden tending would produce great results.

My use of the expression "tend your garden" follows his train of thought. We must tend our minds diligently, year around, constantly being attentive to planting good thoughts, keeping weeds away, clearing clutter, even deliberately allowing our mind to rest and recharge. This task is never concluded. Yet constant diligence can yield big benefits.

Fortunately, gardening isn't about perfection. A person doesn't garden as if they were tabulating a spreadsheet, neatly lining up columns of numbers that balance exactly. Success with a garden is more about producing an overall health and yield. I find great comfort in the words of Jesus describing a similar picture:

> "Take my yoke upon you and learn from me, for I am gentle and humble in heart, and you will find rest for your souls. For my yoke is easy and my burden is light."
> (Matthew 11:29–30)

The whole passage is rich with teaching. One portion I find intriguing is that pedagogical short phrase Jesus used:

"Learn from me."

That means Jesus teaches us. He instructs us little by little, day by day, moment by moment. He informs us how to truly live—what to do, say, hope for, and how to think. Christ is a patient instructor. Although He constantly encourages us toward holiness, He doesn't demand flawlessness from us. He invites us toward honesty and spiritual richness, encouraging us constantly to grow in grace and knowledge of Him. He does this without whipping us like we are horses chained to a chariot in a race. There is no goading from

Jesus. No inciting us to frenzy. Instead, His yoke is easy, and His burden is light.

J. B. Phillips writes,

> It is refreshing, and salutary, to study the poise and quietness of Christ. His task and responsibility might well have driven a man out of his mind. But he was never in a hurry, never impressed by numbers, never a slave of the clock. He was acting, he said, as he observed God to act.[2]

I don't want you to finish this book and feel stressed, worrying that your thought life must be perfectly buttoned down or that you must have it all together immediately. If you mess up one day or entertain an illicit thought for a few moments, remember that verse in Matthew 11 about the easy yoke, and keep learning from Jesus. Consider that His love is steadfast and never ceases. His mercies are new every morning. His faithfulness is great (Lamentations 3:22–23).

Our task is to walk in step with the Holy Spirit, steadily growing in our thought life as in every aspect of spiritual life, mindful of sins and confessing them as they arise, yet constantly filling and refilling our mind with the affections of Christ, allowing God to transform us. Our spiritual life isn't a stage. Jesus isn't part of some imaginary audience, sharply critiquing our performance, applauding our successes, and booing our weaknesses.

Rather, our spiritual life is like an empty wineglass placed upside-down on a table. We are invited to turn it upright, point it toward Heaven, and let Jesus fill it to overflowing with the life-giving

---

[2] J. B. Phillips, *Your God Is Too Small* (New York: Macmillan, 1962), 55.

richness of new wine. Jesus is our savior, guide, friend, and King. He is patient with our shortcomings. He is restorative with our wounds. He is instructive with our pathways. He constantly shines a light before us, showing us the way to go.

With Diligent Ease

An imbalance in the other direction—away from perfection and toward licentiousness—can be equally troubling. I see a grave mistake being made today: when Bible teachers and writers hear of the magnitude of sin in people's lives, they shrug it off, exclaiming, "We're all just messy people. Thank goodness for God's grace!"

Yes, thank goodness for God's grace. I thank Him every day for it. I'm also careful to remember that God is aware of every thought in my mind—and that some of these thoughts can dishonor Him and harm me. I fear we do too much softhearted sympathizing with our propensity to sin. Rather, we're instructed to remember the muscled commands of the Holy Spirit in Scripture: "Prepare your minds for action!" (1 Peter 1:13a NASB). "Stop thinking like children.... In your thinking be adults" (1 Corinthians 14:20). We believers too easily forget Paul's emphatic words at the end of Romans 6:1–2: "What shall we say, then? Shall we go on sinning so that grace may increase? By no means!"

My encouragement for us all is to find the balance of living with the "diligent ease" that comes from walking in step with the Spirit. The two words are chosen carefully. Yes, we must be diligent to shun sin and champion righteousness. Yet there's also a holy relaxation that emerges when we soak ourselves in the truth that God is in control, and our greatest joys and benefits emerge when we are aligned with Christ and His best for our lives. Grace covers all our sins, yet we must never allow the abundance of grace to become an excuse for sin.

As a response to this invitation to live with diligent ease, I encourage us all to follow the instructions of 2 Corinthians 5:9: "We make it our goal to please him."

Focused on the Present

When it comes to the constant tending of our mental garden, the Bible calls us to a dual focus—and that can seem paradoxical. As believers, we're instructed to keep both eyes on the present, while simultaneously fixing both eyes on eternity. Our two-pronged invitation is to be fully attentive to the immediate, while at the same time considering eternal repercussions. Put simply: we must live in the moment while also thinking about the life to come.

Paul surfaced this paradox in Philippians 1:21–26. He kept his attention on two places—Heaven and Earth, the immediacy of the present, and the eternity of Heaven. He was constantly mindful that he had more than one home. He wanted to be with Christ in Heaven. But he also wanted to remain here on Earth so he could fruitfully labor. He wrote:

> For to me, to live is Christ and to die is gain. If I am to go on living in the body, this will mean fruitful labor for me. Yet what shall I choose? I do not know!
>
> I am torn between the two: I desire to depart and be with Christ, which is better by far; but it is more necessary for you that I remain in the body.
>
> Convinced of this, I know that I will remain, and I will continue with all of you for your progress and joy

in the faith, so that through my being with you again
your boasting in Christ Jesus will abound on account
of me.

Believers are sometimes accused of being too heavenly minded. Critics say our heads are stuck in the clouds; we ignore life on Earth because we're only concerned with the afterlife. This criticism carries some weight. If we ignore issues of justice here on Earth because we're only concerned about life in Heaven, then we have forgotten important groups of people Jesus cares for—the poor, the oppressed, the downtrodden, and the marginalized.

Still, I encourage us to become and stay as heavenly minded as possible, because the Bible doesn't present the dual task of being heavenly minded and earthly minded as an "either-or" arrangement. Rather, it's "both-and." Our eyes stay fixed on Heaven, and our eyes stay focused on Earth. We know of this dual focus from passages such as the second stanza of the Lord's Prayer, Matthew 6:10 (KJV):

Thy kingdom come. Thy will be done on earth, as it is
in heaven.

Here, Jesus encourages us to pray for the diligent rule and reign of God on Earth, just like it's done in Heaven. We are asking God that His will would be "both-and"—on Earth and Heaven, in the focus on the present, in the awareness of eternity.

Note this same kind of dual-focus prayer expressed by King David in Psalm 16:11 ESV when he says: "You make known to me the path of life; in your presence there is fullness of joy; at your right hand are pleasures forevermore."

David is acknowledging both the present joy of knowing God and the pleasures that await him forevermore. He is confident in his assertions, not guessing about how to live each day. His plan calls to live each day with the diligence of walking in step with the Lord each moment. Yet David is keeping his eyes on the future, too. He knows the life to come is greater than the life here and now.

How can we grasp this same dual focus? How can we be fully present in each moment God has for us while constantly keeping our eyes on eternity also?

First, we want to let our yes be yes (Matthew 5:37) and live from that decisiveness. Being mentally present in a situation means we have agreed to be there. We are committed to the moment.

Dinnertime with family or friends is a prime example of when intentionality is required. It can be easy to be mentally absent from loved ones because we're rehashing what went on during the day in our mind. Yet when we sit with our family, we can gently remind ourselves that our yes means yes. We have said yes to dinner, and we've said yes to our family, so as part of an integrity-filled mindset, we want to be mentally present at the table.

Second, respecting the Sabbath is an important part of being present in the here and now. Simply, if we aren't well rested and recharged, then it can be hard to stay mentally focused on anything. In Mark 6:31, Jesus invited His followers to "Come with me by yourselves to a quiet place and get some rest." That's an invitation to us as well.

Honoring the Sabbath was an Old Testament command that wasn't repeated in the New Testament, yet Jesus still honored the Sabbath, and He always did so with an eye to the greater good. He allowed his hungry friends to pick grain as they walked through a field on the Sabbath (Matthew 12:1–2), because the day was meant for nourishment. He healed a man with a withered hand on the Sabbath (Matthew 12:9–14), because the Sabbath was meant for healing and health. He asserted His authority over all events and purposes of the Sabbath, saying in Mark 2:27–28, "The Sabbath was made for man, not man for the Sabbath. So the Son of Man is LORD even of the Sabbath."

Finally, we acknowledge that each moment of our lives is under the full authority of Jesus Christ. Psalm 118:24 ESV says: "This is the day that the Lord has made; let us rejoice and be glad in it." Meaning: each day is from God, even the difficult ones.

Have you noticed how some days feel like a constant hum of noise? The activities in our lives mix and merge together like the never-ending rush of cars on a freeway. Sirens and horns blare continually. It can be difficult to catch our breath. We need to remind ourselves that this day belongs to the Lord, and that we're called to live in the moments of it. I love how Psalm 116:9 states it: "And so I walk in the LORD's presence as I live here on earth."

That's us. No matter where we are. No matter what we're called to do. No matter what challenges lie on the horizon, we are walking in the Lord's presence. We are thinking in the Lord's presence—here and now. We are living in the Lord's presence—each and every moment.

Thoughts on Eternity

One day, you and I both will finish this race. Do you ever let your thoughts wander to what comes afterward? It's not morbid to think of the afterlife. Rather, it can be comforting, even exciting, and Colossians 3:2 encourages us in this direction. Paul says, "Let heaven fill your thoughts; don't spend your time worrying about things down here" (TLB).

Note the specific phrasing of that first phrase. "Let heaven fill your thoughts," because that's how I want to conclude this book: by offering a strong and extended encouragement this direction.

When our thoughts are filled with heaven, so many struggles in our thought life are done away with. Those thoughts are put into perspective and exchanged for a true and far better affection. It becomes a needful part of our garden tending process: setting our minds and hearts on things above.

I remember as a boy trying to imagine what Heaven would be like. Our pastor talked about Jesus coming back again soon to take us to Heaven, and that seemed like a good thing to me. But I confess that I didn't want Jesus to come back immediately. I still had things on Earth I wanted to do, things that seemed greater than anything Heaven could offer. You know—like getting my driver's license.

How childish that thought seems today. Even so, it's still not easy for me to let Heaven fill my mind. Heaven tends to mix with thoughts of grief. Someone I know has died and gone to Heaven, and I miss him or her. Or I imagine Jesus's return—us circumventing death and the Lord gathering us to meet with Him—but I get lost in trying to figure out exactly how that's going to work.

Scripture is clear that Jesus will return soon. Maybe today. Maybe two seconds from now. The point of Scripture's teaching on end times is not that we be confused, argumentative, or shirk our responsibilities here and now. We can continually wonder and endlessly debate when and how the return will happen, instead of seeing the wonder and beauty held out to us in 1 Thessalonians 4:16–18.

> For the Lord himself will come down from heaven, with a loud command, with the voice of the archangel and with the trumpet call of God, and the dead in Christ will rise first.

After that, we who are still alive and are left will be caught up together with them in the clouds to meet the Lord in the air. And so we will be with the Lord forever.

Therefore encourage one another with these words.

Did you catch the last line? We are going to be with the Lord forever, so the invitation is to "encourage one another with these words." We are not to be confused by the words. We are not to be afraid of the words. We are not to debate the words. We are to let these words fill our hearts with great hope. We are to talk about this promise to others in the spirit of encouragement. Jesus is coming again soon! That's going to be an incredible thing!

Three passages of Scripture reassure us of our eternal destination. First John 5:12 tells us that when Christ is in our life, we can know without a doubt we have eternal life with Him. Great confidence lies in John's words. Paul in 2 Corinthians 5:8 affirms the same thing: "Yes, we are fully confident, and we would rather be away from these earthly bodies, for then we will be at home with the Lord" (NLT). In Philippians 1:23, Paul adds that he desires "to depart and be with Christ, which is better by far."

From those three passages, we see that after we die, we will be absent from our earthly bodies, at least until we are given resurrected bodies (see 1 Corinthians 15:35–49). Yet being absent from a body doesn't mean we stop existing. Rather, physical death means that the immaterial part of us will move from one place to another. Our new destination will be "at home with the Lord"—which is better by far than this earth. We don't need to doubt these matters. We can be certain. The Bible indicates we can know for sure that we have eternal life—and that eternal life will be wonderful.

Let's allow our minds to go there as we close this book. Let's deliberately let Heaven fill our thought life. What might this eternal life with the Lord be like?

Well, I wish I could tell you exactly. Paul grapples with this difficulty in 1 Corinthians 2:9. He tries to describe Heaven, but all he can muster is this: "No eye has seen, no ear has heard, and no mind has imagined what God has prepared for those who love him" (NLT).

Beyond that, the Bible gives us only a few hints. John, in Revelation 21, mentions new heavens and a new Earth. He describes a brilliant, multidimensional city that shines with the glory of God, and adds that God "will wipe every tear from [our] eyes. There will be no more death or mourning or crying or pain, for the old order of things has passed away."

The writer of Hebrews also mentions this city. He calls it "a better country" (Hebrews 11:16) and refers to it as "the heavenly Jerusalem." He describes a spectacular place where multitudes of redeemed people join "thousands upon thousands of angels in joyful assembly" (Hebrews 12:22–23).

Revelation 7:9–10 gives us a further glimpse into this wondrous multiethnic assembly—people "from every nation, tribe, people, and language, standing before the throne and before the Lamb." We are all crying out in the same loud voice, "Salvation belongs to our God, who sits on the throne, and to the Lamb!"

Let Heaven fill your thoughts. Wow, I wish I could better describe to you what it will be like—but I think that's part of eternity's attraction. The writers of Scripture, even under the inspiration of the Holy Spirit, struggled with the right words to get our minds around what it will be like. They struggled because the concepts simply aren't translatable yet to people on Earth. Heaven offers categories for living that don't yet connect to our earthly minds.

So we need to move beyond our categories. We need to root ourselves in Scripture and let our imaginations run for a bit. When we do, perhaps we can think of eternity more like this…

I Wish I Could Tell You

Start by considering the three main stages of life.[3] The first stage is in the womb. It lasts nine months. The second stage arrives after you're born. It's life on Earth from cradle to grave. The third stage is eternity. It lasts forever.

In the first stage of life, the womb, you have an awareness of life, but it's a very limited understanding. You can see with your eyes, but only darkness and light. You can't hear very much—only the muffled sounds from the outside world. You are nourished, but you can eat only that which passes to you through your umbilical cord from your mother. You can move, but only to roll over, yawn, stretch, wave a hand, or kick a foot. In terms of traveling any distance, you can only go wherever your mother takes you. Life can be full and rich inside the womb, but it's not as full and rich as it's going to be in the future—in the second stage of life, after you are born.

Imagine talking to a baby inside the womb. You put your mouth close to the belly of a pregnant woman and try to describe what the second stage of life will be like. The baby has no vocabulary for it yet. No categories for picturing what the future will hold. Nothing to compare it with.

Outside the womb, a child will see new and wonderful colors, shapes, patterns, and friendly faces. He'll meet his parents face to face and be able to enjoy their love in new and up-close ways. He'll

---

[3] We're grateful to Chaplain Fr. Norm Supancheck for offering the analogy of the three stages of life.

have brothers and sisters, aunts and uncles, and grandparents who will absolutely go nuts with their cameras when they meet him for the first time. As he grows, he'll make friends at church and school and will be able to play baseball and soccer and ride a skateboard. Imagine trying to describe to a baby inside the womb what a bicycle is like. Or a university. Or a rollercoaster. The categories just aren't there yet.

One day, the child inside the womb will hear the music of the piano, of guitars and strings and saxophones and drums. She'll make time to dance with one hand waving free.

The child will meet other living beings—animals, we call them—and they'll interact with her in fun and surprising ways. She'll meet friendly dogs and purring cats. She'll keep a turtle in her room. She'll gallop on a horse over wild, open terrain. She'll laugh at playful parakeets. She'll swim with dolphins.

The child will use vehicles to travel to amazing places. She'll ride on mountain bikes and in speedboats and in a classic 1957 Chevy and inside supersonic jets. She'll journey to the mountains, to the beach, to New York City, Bombay, and Rome.

She will taste a bowl of chocolate ice cream, a piping hot pepperoni pizza, the crisp tang of an orange. She'll blow out candles on a birthday cake and make a wish.

That child in the womb simply is not able to grasp the wonder that awaits. And yet the wonder does await!

Can you see where I'm going with this?

The third stage of life comes after we die, or after the Lord returns to take us home forever. Eternity is every bit as real as the first two stages of life. We don't have the categories yet to grasp what it will be like. All we know is that "no eye has seen, no ear has heard, no mind has conceived, what God has prepared for those who love him." Based on that verse alone, we know that one day we will be in an amazing place beyond anything we can currently imagine. Oh, I wish I could describe it to you. To myself.

One day we will live in supernatural, multidimensional mansions made of gold—celestial homes that provide a wondrous mix of community and solitude, sanctuary and opportunity, exactly what we need. We will inhabit a new country of sights and sounds and smells and tastes and experiences.

One day, we will reunite with our loved ones and meet believers who have gone before us—and we'll be able to interact with them in new ways. Our loved ones won't be aging anymore, infirm in any way, riddled with cancer, or forgetting our names because of Alzheimer's. We will run with our grandparents. We will climb trees with Adam and Eve.

We will hear the Lord's voice. We will meet Jesus face to face. We will ride on the winds of the Holy Spirit. What will meeting God possibly be like?

I'm fairly sure we will taste heavenly food. There won't be any more hunger and thirst in Heaven (Revelation 7:16). Jesus ate a piece of broiled fish with His resurrected body (Luke 24:42–43). Revelation 22:2 mentions a tree of life "bearing twelve crops of fruit, yielding its fruit every month." We know we're going to have at least one incredible meal at "the marriage supper of the Lamb" (Revelation 19:9).

We will dance to the music of angels. We know there will be singing (Revelation 4:8) and instruments (Revelation 5:8–9). It won't be the kind of music that puts you to sleep or the kind that divides people because of individual musical tastes. It will be music that fills us with the spectacular.

What kind of heavenly beings might we meet and interact with? Perhaps the fiery six-winged seraphim who surround God's throne and cry out "holy, holy, holy" (Isaiah 6:2–6). Maybe the four-winged cherubim described in Ezekiel 10:20–21. Will we converse with the chief warrior-angel Michael (Revelation 12:7)? Will we sit down to dine with the messenger-angel Gabriel, asking him all about the time he told the virgin Mary she was going to have a child (Luke 1:26–38)?

Our days won't be boring. Heaven isn't about lying around on clouds. We will have new and purposeful activities; work was part of God's original plan, and He designed it to be good and fulfilling.

In the spirit of the Sabbath, we'll probably have new types of recreation, rest, excitement, and fun. Will there be art galleries in Heaven? What kind of amusement parks might exist on the new Earth?

I wonder if we will have new kinds of vehicles that transport us from place to place. Perhaps we'll move around to different parts of the new heavens and Earth. Perhaps we'll travel to different universes. Perhaps, using imagery envisioned by C. S. Lewis, we'll be able to swim up waterfalls and run forever at great speed without growing tired.

The things we will experience for eternity will be so vastly different from what we experience today. There will be no more pain in that reality. No more sickness in our new home. No more heartache. No more suffering or sorrow.

Instead, there will be perfect understanding. Perfect communication. Perfect relationships. Perfect peace. Perfect joy. Perfect purpose. Perfect fulfillment. Perfect excitement. Perfect fun.

Let your mind go there—to a place that you don't have categories for yet. That's one way you can let Heaven fill your thoughts. And since your mind is filled with Heaven, the second part of Colossians 3:2 NLT emerges in its importance. Paul says, "Don't spend your time worrying about things down here."

When our thoughts are filled with Heaven, we are far slower to take offense with other people and far quicker to extend forgiveness when it's called for. Offenses are real, but in light of eternity, we are able to have a larger perspective. When we think about Heaven, we can let go of our usual annoyances. We can rid ourselves of any grudge we might harbor. We can welcome people anew and let forgiveness flow.

When we think about Heaven, we can live out the words of Hebrews 10:24: "Let us consider how we may spur one another on toward love and good deeds." In light of eternity, tasks have different values. We live in the here and now, yet we live with our thoughts in eternity. We remember that life on Earth is short, and although it is important, Heaven awaits.

When our thoughts are filled with Heaven, we can remind ourselves of the promises and comfort of John 14, where Jesus says,

> "Do not let your hearts be troubled. My Father's house has many rooms; if that were not so, would I have told you that I am going there to prepare a place for you? And if I go and prepare a place for you, I will come back and take you to be with me that you also may be where I am. You know the way to the place where I am going."

Best of all, in eternity, we will see God and know Him in ways we can't yet imagine. First John 3:2 makes this clear. "We know that when Christ appears...we shall see him as he is."

Yes, the minefields of the mind are present for today. Our thought lives are assaulted with the things of this world. But the minefields don't need to destroy us. We can fill our minds with thoughts from above, the affections of Christ, the thoughts of God. We can dwell on all things true and noble and right and good. For the glory and renown of God, it's a new quality of life for us today and a taste of the life to come.

Key Takeaways

- A healthy lifelong practice is the constant cultivation of your mind. You plant good thoughts, keep weeds away, clear clutter, and allow your mind to rest and recharge. This task is never concluded. Yet the constant diligence can yield big benefits.
- As believers, we're instructed to keep both eyes on the present, while both eyes stay fixed on eternity. Our invitation is to be fully attentive to the immediate, yet we're also directed to keep eternity constantly in view. Put simply: we must live in the moment while also thinking about the life to come.
- We live in the moment by letting our yes be our yes, by mentally committing to be present where we are. We live in eternity by filling our thoughts with heaven, which can sometimes require a bit of imagination. Ultimately, when we remember that heaven awaits, that helps us live here and now.

Quick Guide

(Cut out this sheet and place it in a readily accessible place)

Thoughts Matter
(Matthew 5:27–28)

Go to Your God-Thought
(Hebrews 12:1–2)

I Am a New Creation
(2 Corinthians 5:17)

Captive! Get Out, in Jesus's Name!
(2 Corinthians 10:5, Philippians 4:8)

Uncover, Lament, Pray to Go Forward
(Lord, what do you want me to do in this situation?)
(James 1:5)

Shout for Truth!
(John 8:31–32)

I Want to Get Well!
(John 5:1–5)

My Sexual Thoughts Don't Run Wild
(Song of Solomon 8:8–10)

Let Heaven Fill Your Thoughts
(Colossians 3:2 TLB)

Acknowledgements

Thanks to Timothy Peterson, Karla Dial, and the entire team at Salem Books. Greg Johnson at WordServe Literary. The entire team at NewLife Ministries. David Kopp, for your excellent feedback. Early readers Hazel C. Jones, Bob Craddock, Dorothy Brotherton, and David Graham.

About the Authors

STEPHEN ARTERBURN is the founder and chairman of New-Life Ministries and host of the #1 nationally syndicated Christian counseling talk show *NewLife Live!*, heard and watched by over two million people each week.

A *New York Times* bestselling author, Stephen is the developer and editor of eighteen specialty and study Bibles, three of which were nominated for Bible of the Year. The *Spiritual Renewal Bible* ___ the award.

___ ___hen's bestselling books include *Every Man's Battle*, *Toxic* ___ *It for Life*, and *Healing Is a Choice*. *The Life Recovery* ___ d more than three million copies, and *Every Man's* ___ nationally bestselling study Bible. Altogether, Stephen ___ million books in print and has received four Gold ___ "Book of the Year" awards, including an ECPA Gold ___ on of excellence for the children's book *Kirby McCook and* ___ *esus Chronicles*, written with M. N. Brotherton.

Stephen has studied at Texas A&M University, Newburgh Theological Seminary, and Southwestern Baptist Theological Seminary. He has earned degrees from Baylor University and the University of North Texas. One of his honorary doctorates is from the California Graduate School of Theology. He serves as the Teaching Pastor at Northview Church in Carmel, Indiana, where he lives with his wife, Misty, and their family.

M. N. BROTHERTON is a *New York Times* bestselling author and coauthor dedicated to writing books that inspire heroics, promote empathy, and encourage noble living. He often writes books in conjunction with high-profile public figures, humanitarians, thought leaders, and military personnel.

Most recently, he was the writing partner for Louie Giglio on two national bestsellers: *Don't Give the Enemy a Seat at Your Table* and *Goliath Must Fall*. With faith-based collaborations, he has also written with Dr. Wayne Cordeiro, Francis Chan, Robert Morris, Doug Fields, Carole Lewis, Martha Hawkins, Jim Putman, Matt Carter, and Neil Tomba.

He has a bachelor's degree from Multnomah University in Portland, Oregon, and a master's degree from Talbot School Theology at Biola University in Los Angeles, where he gr with high honors. He lives with his wife and three ch Pacific Northwest.